I HAVE
A SECULAR VISION

"*God has no religion*"
Gandhi

"*We don't need religion. Period*"
Samuel Butler (2018)

Front and back cover designs by Fabián Gutiérrez

Interior pages editing and formatting by Fabián Gutiérrez

DEDICATION

This book is dedicated to the dawn of a new secular non-religious future where all of humanity grabs destiny by its horns, and bravely, like a hamster on a treadmill, courageously, realizing it is on a spinning cage, boldly leaps out and off to a positive shining new freedom future without the shackles of religion holding it back..

TABLE OF CONTENTS

ACKNOWLEDGMENTS

For persistent, tireless help on art work for the front and back cover, and for research ,editing and formatting and some important content ideas, including researching Secular Declarations, many thanks to Fabián Gutiérrez, Master's Degree in Computer Science.

For the chapter 12, "The forged origins of the New Testament", I'm supremely grateful to its author, Tony Bushby and Nexus Magazine for allowing me to use this revealing chapter in its entirely.

CHAPTER 1

GOD HAS NO RELIGION

THINK!!, if we didn't have religion, we wouldn't have had:

- ❖ The Crusades , where Christians burned alive Jews and Muslims together in Jerusalem.
- ❖ The Inquisition, which lasted over 400 years.
- ❖ The Salem witch hangings.
- ❖ The "30 year War" between Protestants and Catholics
- ❖ The violence and killings in Ireland between Catholics and Protestants.
- ❖ The conflict between Hindus and Moslems, in India, including the formation of two states, India and Pakistan.
- ❖ The assassination of the source of the above quote "God has no Religion", Mahatma Gandhi.
- ❖ The killings in Iraq between Sunnis and Shias.
- ❖ The killings in Afghanistan between Sunnis and Shias.
- ❖ The Holocaust.
- ❖ The turmoil presently in the Mid-East between Israel and Palestine.
- ❖ The possible war between Israel, the United States, and Iran.
- ❖ If there were no organized religion, none of the above would have happened.

Think of it. None of the above.

> This Is my simple religion. There is no need for temples; no need for complicated philosophy. Our own brain, our own heart is our temple; the philosophy is kindness." Dalai Lama

> "More violence has occurred in the name of religion than for any other reason." Deepak Chopra in New York Times Bestseller "The Book of Secrets"

> "Religion is something we can perhaps do without." - Dalai Lama From his book Ethics for the New Millennium

CHAPTER 2
BEST CLASS AT UNIVERSITY

Probably the best class that I took at the University of California at Berkeley was a speech class from Professor Telfer. It turned out to be much more than about speechmaking.

In one of the first classes, he pointed to someone in the class, almost at random it seemed – "What religion are you?" Even today, one doesn't pry that sharply into the internal beliefs of anyone. You don't touch the subject of religion or politics (politics was next!) in polite society, out of the blue, like that.

A student answered "Catholic", or was it "Protestant", I don't remember right now, but it was one. Let's assume the student said "Catholic".

"Why are you a Catholic?" Telfer asked. "Are your parents Catholic?" The student said "Yes". "Have you investigated any other religion? , he pursued further. "No" was the answer.

"Don't you think you should?" This was a step toward a secular direction for me, and it would be for anybody who becomes a free thinker at this point.

CHAPTER 3
HOW MUCH DOES RELIGION COST?

What is Sukkot?

Sukkot (Feast of Booths or Tabernacles) is one of the three biblically based pilgrimage holidays known as the shalosh regalim. It is an agricultural festival that originally was considered a thanksgiving for the fruit harvest. Sukkot are hut-like structures that the Jews lived in during the 40 years of travel through the wilderness after the exodus from Egypt. As a temporary dwelling, the sukkah also represents the fact that all existence is fragile, and therefore Sukkot is a time to appreciate the shelter of our homes and our bodies.

How is Sukkot celebrated?

Sukkot is celebrated by, first of all, building a sukkah. Jews are required to eat in the sukkah for eight days (seven days in Israel), and some even sleep in the sukkah for the duration of the holiday. The sukkah is decorated and the first day is considered a holy day in which most forms of work are forbidden. The rabbis dictated that arbat ha'minim (four species) should be held together and waved during the holiday. These are based on four plants mentioned in the Bible, and the rabbinic version includes the following: etrog (fruit of the citron tree), lulav (palm frond), hadas (leaves from the myrtle tree), and aravah (leaves from the willow tree). This waving ceremony was performed at the Temple in the ancient world.

The seventh day of Sukkot is called Hoshanah Rabah. On that day in the synagogue Jews circle the room seven times while the arbat ha'minim are held and special prayers are recited.

What kinds of foods are eaten on Sukkot?

There are no traditional Sukkot foods, except for kreplach (stuffed dumplings). Sukkot meal inspiration can come from the harvest origin of the holiday, and meals can include fresh fruits and vegetables, or other harvest-related ingredients. Of course, challah, chicken soup, and kugels are traditional Jewish foods that can be served on Sukkot (or any time of the year).

What is the proper greeting for Sukkot?

To wish someone a Happy Sukkot, simply say "Chag Sameach!" (Happy Holiday).

When is Sukkot?

On the Hebrew calendar, Sukkot starts on the 15th of Tishrei and continues until the 21st of Tishrei.

Sukkot occurs on the following dates:

- ❖ Jewish Year 5779: Sunset September 24, 2018 – Nightfall October 2, 2018

- ❖ Jewish Year 5780: Sunset October 14, 2019 – Nightfall October 22, 2019

- ❖ Jewish Year 5781: Sunset October 3, 2020 – Nightfall October 11, 2020

- ❖ Jewish Year 5782: Sunset September 21, 2021 – Nightfall September 29, 2021

- ❖ Jewish Year 5783: Sunset October 10, 2022 – Nightfall October 18, 2022

From https://toriavey.com

When I first saw the statement in Peter DeRosa's best seller, "Vicars of Christ" that the Vatican Palace had 11,000 rooms, I was sure that I had found a typographical error. Surely he meant to say 11 hundred, which would be enormous enough for a collection of buildings of different periods that cover some 13 1/2 acres (5.5 hectares). Since I had the author's email address, I thought he would welcome this find, if it hadn't already been brought to his attention.

This is how the author responded (within a few hours):

from: Peter DeRosa
To: Ray Dubuque
Sent: Friday, August 20, 2004
Subject: 11,000 Rooms?

Dear Ray,

Some years back, with questions coming at me from all over the world about Vicars of Christ, and having no secretary, I promised myself I would not answer any more questions about that book. If I did I would not be able to write any more. (And he has published several other books since). This is, therefore, by way of an exception to a golden rule!

I seem to remember I first came across a reference to the 11,000 rooms in Zola's novel Rome (1896). It is as much a guide book as a novel, in fact, a marvelously researched guidebook, better than most. I wondered if this was a slip of the pen.

In O Vatican (1984), Paul Hofmann, for 35 years the NYT foreign correspondent, writes, "Nobody seems to know exactly how many rooms the Vatican has, although 12,000 windows have been counted. There are certainly considerably more than 1,000 halls, chambers, chapels, etc."

In Pilgrim Walks in Rome (4th edition 1924), Paul Chandlery SJ writes: "The Vatican is a world in itself. Even those who have visited it can form a very insufficient idea of its immensity. It is not one palace, it is a collection of palaces (museums, art galleries etc) and about 11,000 rooms."

In Ave Roma Immortalis (1928) , F. Marion Crawford writes: "An American lady, on hearing that the Vatican is said to contain 11,000 rooms, threw up her hands and laughingly exclaimed, 'Think of the housemaids!' (In fact, no feminine influence there whatever).

Them, as they say, is me last words on the topic.

Peter

[Now that's my idea of a scholar! Ray Dubuque]

Extracted from http://www.jesuswouldbefurious.org

Religious celebrations

In the Jewish religion when a son or daughter reaches the age of 12 in a Jewish family, there is a celebration called a Bar or Bat Mitzvah . The child reads from a stand , which alone can be a keepsake, and could run thousands of dollars in price. Relatives and friends are invited and sometimes is done in a special place, such as a room in a fancy hotel.

Quinceañera christian daughter introduced to Christian Society when she turns 15.

Instead of paying money for expensive religious events, skip having the event or spending the full cost , and spend only ½ of what you were planning to spend, saving significant money, and spend the saved money on assisting the poor, or making it a gift to a needy relative, or homeless in your area. How about having extra time and money for "family time" and not neglecting your children or other family members.

Inherited wealth and the cost of living Jewish

A September blog post in The Times of Israel, written anonymously by "A Jewish Father" received a lot of attention in the day school world and on social media. Steve Freedman, Head of School at Hillel Day School of Metropolitan Detroit, wrote a well-circulated response on our sister publication JeducationWorld where many chimed in with comments. A comment posted in recent days looks at the cost of day school from an entirely different perspective. We share the comment with you, in full:

DaySchoolParent says:

"It's confusing to me that no one discusses the role of generational wealth in upper middle class Jewish communities. Everyone talks about income and assets but no one mentions the transfer of wealth through down payments, payment for college and graduate school, paying for camp, preschool, weddings, bar mitzvahs, vacations. It's wonderful that Jewish families are willing to help establish their adult children and to pass their wealth down during their lifetimes. But these invisible transfers are rarely fully accounted for in tuition calculations.

If I make the same income as Person A but Person A has no debt and Person A's parents are helping to pay for preschool and Person A also received a down payment from her grandparents and Person A expects help with college tuition for her kids and to inherit substantial wealth by the time Person A retires, Person A has a lot of invisible assets that are not on the form. I may make the same income and have the same housing cost as Person A but we are not in the same class.

Truly middle class people pay for everything they need and their children need from their salaries. There is no expected help from outside sources – you're it. It's up to you to create and earn everything you need and everything you want to give your child.

If day school means that neither Person A nor I will have much extra money, that's actually fine for Person A because if the car breaks down, it will be taken care of, if there is a medical emergency, it will be taken care of, and if the kids need anything, it will be taken care of. If a lot of money were unexpectedly needed, some stock or real estate held by the extended family can always be sold. Person A may not have thousands of dollars in her savings account but her extended family has access to tens of thousands of dollars for the right kinds of expenses.

In contrast, I have to save for my children's college and pay for the bar mitzvah on my own and for summer camp and for orthodontia and for everything else my children might need. If I can't save because I give almost all of my extra income to the day school, then I am passing down my class problems to the next generation instead of building wealth so that my child might someday be more like Person A. Most responsible middle class people still have debt. Financial aid calculations assume that you will make minimum payments on your debt. If I do that, how will I ever get out of debt?

So let's talk about values. Does it make sense for me to put myself into a situation of ongoing financial instability simply because I really want to give my child an intensive Jewish environment? Shouldn't I really be saving my extra income and then paying the dentist and the mechanic and getting ready for the bar mitzvah and for college? Isn't that exactly how Person A's family became the people that can now afford to help Person A? I mean ... most Jews are not descended from European royalty or slave traders.

Maybe day schools – even with financial aid – are an elite experience that is really meant for the children and grandchildren of someone who made it, regardless of the income on the form. Those of us descended from the Jews who never really made it should perhaps be trying harder to improve our lives economically instead of trying harder to fit in with the Jews who already have.

Basic rules of getting ahead: work hard, save money, don't buy things you can't afford. Jewish life has become a very expensive commodity. Maybe those of us who can't afford it should create our own communities instead of continuing to use other people's.

From JewishPhilanthropy.com

CHAPTER 4
A DAY IN THE LIFE
OF A BENEDICTINE MONK

A hard day's night

As a monk in the middle ages following the Rule of St. Benedict, your life was a punishing regime of prayer, reading and manual labour. Monastic life differed amongst the orders. The Cistercians observed an even stricter regime than the Benedictines.

Your daily routine (horarium) was based on the rising and setting of the sun and changed with the seasons; this routine follows the winter timetable.

2.00AM
Wake up for Vigils/nocturns
Monks in the chapel.
You are awoken by ringing of bells, signaling the night office of Vigils.

By candlelight, you chant in unison, sing psalms and say prayers for the dead. It's hard to stay awake and some monks suck on peppercorns to try and stop themselves nodding off. After the service, Benedictine monks have a quick snooze - Cistercians, on the other hand, are afforded no such luxury and read or pray.

7.00am
Back to church for Lauds
Monks sing.

As the sun rises, it is time for Lauds - a service at daybreak which symbolizes Christ's resurrection.

After Lauds, those who are priests celebrate private masses, while the others read in the cloister. As you and your fellow monks read aloud, there's an audible hum. It is believed reading aloud helps you to concentrate on the words.

8:00AM
Scrub up

Monks washes feet.

After another short service which is known as Prime, it's time for you to wash your face and hands and get changed into your day shoes.

You wear a habit which consists of a simple tunic, a hood known as a cowl and a belt. An apron-like garment (scapula) is worn when you are working. Traditionally monastic habits were black, a sign of humility. However, the Cistercians wore habits of undyed wool to proclaim their poverty since dyes were expensive.

8.30am
Study hard
Monk transcribing text.

You now have time for reading or study.

You read theological and classical texts, and transcribe them to preserve knowledge for future generations. Three hours after sunrise you attend the service of Terce where you ask the Holy Spirit for strength in dealing with the conflicts of your day.

10.00am
Confess your sins
Penitent monk.

You go to the Chapter meeting held in the chapter house and confess your sins.

The meeting begins with a prayer, after which the Rule of St Benedict is read out. You are then invited to admit your faults and atone for them. Anyone who does not voluntarily confess is reported and punished.

10.30am
Work hard

Two monks toil in the fields.

The prior bangs on a wooden board to summon the brethren to the parlour.

It's time to carry out your weekly chores around the monastery. Monks in Cistercian monasteries have a harder time and are required to do hard manual labour. At midday, you go to another brief service, Sext, where you remember Christ's crucifixion.

1.30PM
Eat dinner
Monks sit down for dinner.

After None, a short service where you commemorate the death of Christ, it's time for dinner.

You wash your hands before entering the refectory . Your meal consists of a choice of two cooked dishes made from cereal and vegetables, perhaps with a bit of added fish, egg or cheese and a third dish of fruit or vegetables. You have to be silent in the refectory and listen to the reader while you eat. In summer, you have a siesta after the meal before going back to study in the cloister. A light supper is served in summer to sustain you through the longer days.

4.00PM
Attend Vespers
Monks sing by candle light.

At dusk, you gather for Vespers. As the sky grows dark the monks light candles in the church to ward off the darkness.

The lighting of the lamps echoes ancient Jewish rites described in the Old Testament which were performed in the Temple. This very solemn service is also known as Evensong. Again you chant in unison and sing psalms.

4.30PM
Drink a cup of ale
Monk drinks beer.

You drink a cup of ale and then listen to a Collations reading.

The abbot reads from the "Conferences of the Desert Fathers" by the fourth-century monk Saint John Cassian. At sunset, you attend the office of Compline which signals the end of the day. From this time silence is observed until the following morning; any essential communication is made using signs.

7.00PM
Get to bed
Sleeping monks.

At last, you retire to bed. You sleep in a large dormitory, alongside your brothers.

If you change into your night habit you need to take great pains not to expose your body. As you sleep, senior brothers patrol the dorm keeping an eye out for any illicit behaviour. Some monks fear the night as they believe the devil is most active then seeking to lead the sleeping monks astray.

From www.bbc.com

,

CHAPTER 5
THE COST OF BECOMING A PRIEST

What price truth?

The Church spends a good deal of money on the education of priests and religious. From seminary or convent formation to continuing education workshops and retreats, the faithful, of course, bear the cost. In justice, what do the faithful receive in return?

The cost of seminary education is considerable. Room, board and tuition, I'm told, is now something like $40,000 a year per seminarian. That amount is charged to the diocese; it does not include the various gifts and grants seminaries receive, and it is comparable to the overall cost of private college.

Over a typical five-year formation period, the cost of educating a seminarian for the priesthood comes to $200,000. Factoring in the number of seminarians that drop out along the way, the effective cost of educating a single priest rises. A good guess for the cost of priest at the end of the formation assembly line, after quality control rejects, would be something like $250,000, probably more.

I haven't done the math for the formation of sisters (and brothers), and the number may not be as high, unless equivalent college education is included. But the room and board component has to be considerable, and the dropout rate adds to the effective final cost per religious.

(You may be thinking my reducing priests and nuns to financial statistics is unseemly and vulgar, but when I think of my nephew supporting his wife and four kids with three jobs, it just might be useful for priests and religious to recognize the financial burden the Church is placing on him and others like him.)

Add to the overall cost of formation the continuing education costs of the priests or sisters in universities – especially in Rome, the Eternal City – and the overall cost of "the product" continues to rise. We need not continue with this rigorous (if unpleasant) analysis, but I hope the point is well made. The faithful – including my hard-working nephew – bear a considerable cost for their priests and religious. And they deserve value for their hard-earned money.

That question came to mind during a recent overseas tour where I was the designated priest for Mass. In some respects, it was a boondoggle for me. Except for about $500, my expenses were covered by the other members on the tour. (I think it was a fair exchange, though. Despite appearances, there is serious "on-time" pastoral work for such a priest. Hence, I remain unashamed.)

An elderly nun was also on the tour. She didn't look like a nun or expect to be addressed as a nun, nor did she dress like a nun (unless nuns are by rule wearing sneakers and athletic sweat suits nowadays.) She spoke like a nun, however, betraying years of formation, workshops and retreats. Those of us in the trade know: she talked the talk of religion and liturgy. I hoped things would go smoothly and they almost did.

But at the end of the tour, I overheard Sister speaking to a couple of the younger tourists. Sister explained that the future of the Church would be open to those divorced and remarried to give everyone another chance after a failed marriage. (Earlier I'd resolved to navigate the choppy waters of touring with a modern nun by employing silence. I would say nothing about the shameful appearance of our on-a-first-name-basis sister.) We're told that this is, after all, the 21st century.

But now, Sister was talking doctrine. She was opposing the very words of Christ, "What God has joined, let no man put asunder." The spirit of Cardinal Walter Kasper was upon her. But I owed those two young people doctrinal clarity as a matter of justice – and they had paid my freight. Despite my live-and-let-live tactics throughout the tour, I had to intervene.

I told Sister that if the Church's teaching on marriage is going to change, the Church would find it necessary to apologize to Henry VIII, revoke the canonization of Saint Thomas More, rebuke John the Baptist ("The greatest man born of woman"?), canonize Herod and Herodias, and delete the story of Sodom and Gomorrah from the Old Testament. Sister's response was immediate: "I do not believe in doctrine, I believe in love." ("Please stand for the Creed," anyone?) Then she walked off in a huff.

One of the young folks, after Sister's departure, to my delight expressed a renewed confidence in the orthodox Catholic faith and wondered why anyone could think Church teaching could change. For my part, mission accomplished. And I hope I paid for my trip with my jackhammer subtlety.

On the flight home, I reflected about how gloomy it was. A woman dedicated to Christ – a woman who received from lay benefactors a lifetime of pay and benefits, the costs of formation and education – reducing her ministry to an epitaph fitting nicely if sadly on a tombstone: "I do not believe in doctrine, I believe in love."

In return for all the money spent on priests and religious, is it too much to expect that our benefactors receive the faith, the true faith, and nothing but the faith?

By Rev. Jerry J. Pokorsky
From www.thecatholicthing.org

CHAPTER 6
It's too expensive to be Jewish

This spring, my son, Nathaniel, turned 12. It was time to get serious about preparation for his bar mitzvah, which usually happens when a Jewish boy turns 13. We needed to hire a tutor because at the twice-a-month hippie Silver Lake Sunday school my kids attend, Hebrew isn't part of the curriculum. And most bar mitzvah ceremonies include saying blessings on the Torah in Hebrew.

My first call was to the father of a woman I met through taekwondo. Between ax kicks and knife defenses, I had discovered he was a cantor. I figured since she was warm and well-spoken, her dad was probably a good guy. Indeed, he sounded like a mensch. Just what I was looking for. After all, I wanted this to be a positive experience for Nathaniel, not a dull exercise in rote memorization. If things went well, I hoped we would use the same tutor for our daughter when it was time for her bat mitzvah. Then I asked what he charged: $140 per hourlong session.

This is where I should probably note that I am a freelance journalist and my husband works in retail — $140 an hour just isn't in the cards for us. Not once a week, for nearly a year. So I continued my research. I called a man who lived nearby. A stranger I encountered on a local online parenting forum had recommended him, but she was a very enthusiastic stranger. Candidate No. 2 turned out to be the former principal of a Jewish day school — good creds. He too sounded nice when we talked, not at all the stern-principal type. And he charged $80 per session. Never would I have thought I would rejoice over $80 an hour.

For good measure, I decided to reach out to one more person before committing. Not only was she referred by someone I have mad respect for, but she sounded cool, like someone I would want to drink a beer with, if I drank beer. But because she is also a healer who fetches $175 an hour for her services, she requests that same fee for Hebrew lessons. I told her that was a little rich for us.

Why not just join a synagogue, one with a religious school that prepares students for b'nai mitzvah? We used to belong to a synagogue in the San Fernando Valley, not far from where we live. We joined when Nathaniel started preschool there. Like most synagogues with schools, families are required to join the temple and pay the annual membership dues in order to send their child to the school. (Dues aren't a voluntary offering, as is customary in most churches and mosques. School tuition is separate.)

At first it was affordable. But over the years — our daughter attended as well — our annual dues steadily increased, until they were nearly $3,000. Someone in the office there once alluded to this as the elevator system. Or maybe it was the escalator system. All I remember is asking if there were a stairs option.

To be fair, our former temple, like most temples, does offer "financial consideration." We applied for this when our daughter finished preschool, and were offered a few-hundred-dollar reduction in temple dues. But we were still looking at several thousand dollars a year. That did not include religious school, an additional $1,500 or so per kid. My husband and I agreed to move on. Thus the hippie (and way more affordable) Silver Lake Sunday school.

Now, I get that temples have rents and salaries to pay. They are important institutions. And if I could get $175 an hour for doing something other than taking my clothes off — and even that is farfetched, given that the big 5-0 is not too far off — I surely would. But it's expensive to do Jewish. No wonder so many Jews don't. In 2013, the Pew Research Center put the portion of American Jews of no religion, meaning Jews who identify as Jewish by label rather than practice, at 22%. This is triple what it was just a dozen years earlier.

The hefty price tag that comes with being an active Jew surely doesn't help. Just going to High Holiday services — the Rosh Hashanah-Yom Kippur hustle that this year begins Sept. 20 — can set you back a few hundred bucks for tickets. And that's for one person. Oy.

Fortunately, there are organizations working to make Judaism more accessible. IKAR, a spiritual community that gathers in rented space midcity, allows people who can't comfortably swing the standard membership contribution to name their own amount. They call this Ezra membership. They do offer suggested reduced figures based on income. But unlike many temples that require tax returns and financial records before making accommodations, IKAR simply asks that people choose an amount that is "reasonable and meaningful." Nearly one-third of their community are Ezra members.

Temple Ner Simcha, in Westlake Village, took an even bolder step last year, going to a no-dues model, "because it's the righteous and right thing to do," said their spiritual leader, Rabbi Michael Barclay.

"Paying to pray is a concept we as a community simply don't agree with," he added. They still welcome donations of course.

Barclay is the first to admit the change hasn't been easy. But the upside is undeniable. Over 500 Ner Simcha newbies, nearly all of whom were unaffiliated with a temple previously, attended the entirely free High Holiday services last year.

"To make it easy for a Jew to be a Jew," said Barclay. "That's what this is about."

As for Nathaniel, baseball and sleep-away camp and a million other not-so-good excuses have prevented me from setting up his first tutoring session. But it's on my to-do list. Candidate No. 2 for the win.

CHAPTER 7
Reverend Cecil Williams

Reverend Cecil Williams, CEO of Glide Memorial United Methodist Church and Minister of Glide's National and International Ministries, delivered the 2006 commencement address on Saturday, May 13. Reverend Williams also received an honorary doctor of humane letters degree during the ceremonies.

"You have been trained and informed so you can bring hope to the world," Reverend Williams told the graduating class of 2006. "No matter how hopeless it seems, there are people prepared to bring hope into the world and that is why education is so critical. Education builds a community in everything we do." More than 420 students received degrees on May 13. This included 298 undergraduate students and 128 graduate students. This was the largest graduating class in Dominican's 116-year history. On June 3, an additional 118 students graduated from Dominican's teacher credential program.

Rev. Williams encouraged graduates to be liberated and make their own decisions.

"It's important to not just be normal," he said. "We must participate in diversity if we are to have a beloved community."

In his 40 years as Pastor of Glide Memorial United Methodist Church, Reverend Williams has created a church that practices diversity, spirituality, and compassion. As a minister, community leader, author, lecturer, and spokesperson for the poor and marginalized, he is respected and recognized as a national leader on the forefront of social change. Under his leadership, Glide grew to become one of the largest social services providers in San Francisco. His vision for a truly inclusive church has attracted a 11,000-member congregation who reflect the diversity of the world- all races, ages, genders, ethnicities, sexual orientations and religions.

Reverend Williams is married to Janice Mirikitani, Executive Director of Glide's programs and President of the Glide Foundation, and Poet Laureate of San Francisco. Under Janice Mirikitani's direction and Reverend William's leadership, Glide offers more

Under the leadership of Reverend Cecil and Janice, GLIDE has long been the greatest provider of social services that San Francisco has seen. It serves nearly 3,000 meals a day and 850,000 meals a year. GLIDE has also long been a loyal provider of Aids/ HIV screenings … and provider of adult education classes and programs for advancement … and provider of assistance to women challenged with homelessness, domestic violence, substance abuse and mental health issues.

"Cecil and Janice took a dying church and turned it into one of the most important social institutions that I've seen in this country." – Warren Buffett

CHAPTER 8
World's least religious countries

The world's most populous country is also the globe's least religious. According to a new study, 90 percent of all Chinese consider themselves to be atheists or not to be religious.

The survey of 65 countries, conducted by Gallup International and the WI Network of Market Research, is based on 63,898 interviews. China tops the list of the world's least religious nations by far; it's followed by countries in Europe — about three fourth of all Swedish and Czech also said that they were either atheists or not religious.

Although China's society has deep religious traditions, decades of Communist rule have installed a widespread atheistic materialism that still surprises many visitors.

Sweden's top spot among the world's least religious nations is astonishing, as well. The Scandinavian country has increasingly become more secular in recent years and observers have noticed a disconnect between the popularity of religious traditions such as Christmas or Easter and true religious commitment.

Only eight percent of all Swedes regularly attend religious services, according to the Swedish government. Its Web site provides further explanations why the nation is much less religious than its neighbors.

Least religious countries

Percentage of respondents in each country claiming to be either not religious or atheist

Source: WIN/Gallup International

The Washington Post

With its high numbers of atheist citizens, China and Hong Kong appear to be outliers in Asia. Western Europe and Oceania are the only regions where about 50 percent of the population or more either consider themselves to be atheists or not religious, as well.

In Western Europe, the U.K. and the Netherlands top the ranking, followed by Germany, Switzerland, Spain and Austria. In France, about half of the population is not religious or atheist — despite the fact that it is generally considered to be the birthplace of Western secularism.

With 65 percent, Israel has surprisingly many citizens who consider themselves not religious or to be atheists. According to Israeli newspaper Haaretz, atheism is deeply entrenched in the country's society. Many Jews furthermore practice some religious acts, but consider themselves as secular. In the West Bank and Gaza, only 19 percent of all respondents said that they were not religious.

Countries with large numbers of atheists

Percentage of respondents in each country claiming to be either not religious or atheist.

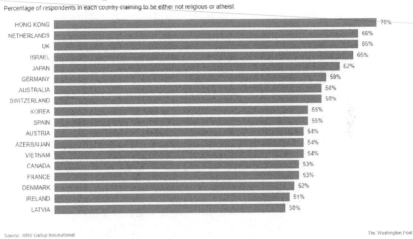

HONG KONG	70%
NETHERLANDS	66%
UK	65%
ISRAEL	65%
JAPAN	62%
GERMANY	59%
AUSTRALIA	58%
SWITZERLAND	58%
KOREA	55%
SPAIN	55%
AUSTRIA	54%
AZERBAIJAN	54%
VIETNAM	54%
CANADA	53%
FRANCE	53%
DENMARK	52%
IRELAND	51%
LATVIA	50%

Source: WIN/ Gallup International   The Washington Post

The study also sheds light at other differences in religious habits that are unrelated to national borders. The survey's authors found that people younger than 34 tend to be more religious than older respondents. This is particularly surprising from a U.S. perspective where an increasing number of younger citizens do not identify with any religion at all — contrary to older Americans.

The researchers also examined other variables apart from age. "Those without what is considered an education are the most religious but religious people are a majority in all educational levels," they concluded.

According to their analysis, education plays a smaller role in determining the religiousness of an individual than income. "Among those with a medium high and high income less than 50 percent say they are religious, against 70 percent of those with low, medium low and medium income."

This observation reflects an earlier study by the Pew Research Center which found that a country's level of religiosity tracks closely with a nation's GDP per capita. In other words: Richer countries also tend to be less religious than poorer nations. The only outliers of this observation were China and the United States.

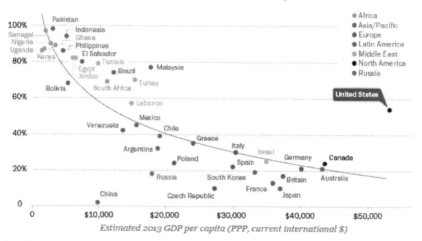

Wealthier Nations Tend to Be Less Religious, But U.S. a Prominent Exception

% saying religion plays a very important role in their lives (2011-2013)

Note: The curve represents the logarithmic relationship between GDP per capita and the percentage saying that religion plays a very important role in their lives. Germany, France, Britain % data from spring 2011; U.S., Japan % data from spring 2012. Source: Spring 2011, 2012, 2013 Global Attitudes survey. Data for GDP per capita (PPP) from IMF World Economic Outlook Database, April 2014.

PEW RESEARCH CENTER

This list of the world's least religious nations does not indicate a decline of belief. Worldwide, six out of 10 people say that they are religious. Most believers can be found in Africa and the Middle East where eight out of 10 people would consider themselves to be religious, followed by Eastern Europe, America and Asia.

"With the trend of an increasingly religious youth globally, we can assume that the number of people who consider themselves religious will only continue to increase," Jean-Marc Leger, president of Win/Gallup International, was quoted as saying by the British

Guardian newspaper.

Among the 65 countries surveyed by Gallup International, Thailand led the list of the most religious nations with 94 percent of the population considering itself to be religious. Armenia, Bangladesh, Georgia and Morocco followed Thailand in the ranking.

From https://www.washingtonpost.com

CHAPTER 9
What does Darwin say?
He has already spoken

Darwin letter reveals, "I do not believe in the Bible"

While many scholars believe Charles Darwin was an agnostic or even an atheist, it can be difficult to find hard evidence to back up those beliefs. He was reluctant to discuss religion and his writings are often silent on the issue.

But now a simple one-sentence handwritten letter signed by the naturalist offers proof he did not believe in God. The letter, written 21 years after the publication of "The Origin of Species," will be auctioned off Monday afternoon at Bonhams in New York. It fetched $197,000 at the auction, three times the previous record of $59,142 for a four-page letter that Darwin had penned to his niece.

Darwin's letter is a reply to a young barrister named Francis McDermott, who wrote on November 23, 1880 with a very unusual request: "...If I am to have pleasure in reading your books I must feel that at the end I shall not have lost my faith in the New Testament. My reason in writing to you therefore is to ask you to give me a Yes or No to the question Do you believe in the New Testament." McDermott continues by promising not to publicize Darwin's reply in the "theological papers."

The next day Darwin responded. He wasn't brusque but he was to the point and left no doubt about his beliefs, stating: "Dear Sir, I am sorry to have to inform you that I do not believe in the Bible as a divine revelation & therefore not in Jesus Christ as the son of God. Yours faithfully."

McDermott promised not to publish the correspondence and he kept to his word. The letter was unknown to scholars for over 100 years.

"He has no hesitation about it. He doesn't beat around the bush," Cassandra Hatton, director of Bonhams history of science and technology department, told CBS News. "He is direct about what he thinks. It's a one-sentence letter. He doesn't try to make the young man feel better or make an apology. He just directly says I'm sorry to inform you that I don't believe in the Bible. It's very clear."

Matthew Chapman, the great-great grandson of Darwin who is also the president of sciencedebate.org, a group is trying to persuade the final presidential candidates to have a debate on science and technology, said Darwin may have been open about his beliefs in the letter because he was approaching death.

"You have to remember this was written two years before he died," Chapman told CBS News. "I don't think you screw around with this kind of stuff. You say what mean. I don't think you are inclined to lie or showboat. You know you are facing death at that point and so I think this is a clear and honest expression of his atheism."

Chapman said he found Darwin's response enlightening given the highly charged nature of the issue.

"The guy who wrote the letter was asking, should I read your work or will it challenge my faith? I think that is as interesting as Darwin's response," he said. "This guy is saying, if there is anything that challenges what I believe already I don't want to hear it. In that context, Darwin's reply was pretty kind."

Darwin grew up going to church and studied theology at Christ's College, Cambridge. But his views began to change after he took his history-making voyage on the Beagle. He returned to write "The Origin of Species" in 1859, the book that would detail his theory of evolution through natural selection. It sparked huge debate in Victorian England and prompted questions over Darwin's religions views.

Darwin rarely discussed religion, probably to respect the feelings of his friends and family. Just a month before penning this note, Darwin wrote to the prominent atheist Edward Aveling, "It has ... been always my object to avoid writing on religion, and I have confined myself to science."

Darwin died in 1882. Rumors of a deathbed conversion were widely believed but firmly denied by his daughter.

"Many people theorized he changed his mind towards the ends of life and there has been speculation about a deathbed conversion," Hatton said. "But this letter again is late in his life. That would kind of throw doubt on the conjecture that Darwin did believe in God towards the end of his life."

Darwin remains a deeply polarizing figure today and is despised among those who believe in creationism, the theory that God had a hand in evolution.

"I find his atheism interesting. When you balance that against his scientific achievements which were so rigorous and so detailed and so prolific, it should be a fairly small thing," Chapman said. "Certainly in England and Europe, this wouldn't be much off an issue. He was a great scientist and this was the conclusion he came to."

Along with the Darwin letter, the auction sold several other items important to the history of science. Among them was a Apple-1 computer, the first pre-assembled personal computer to come to market. It is in mint condition and was estimated to go for as much as $500,000. Details of the winning bid were not available.

There was also Nobel Prize medal awarded to George Minot in 1934 for his pioneering work on the treatment of pernicious anemia that went for $545,000 as well as a prototype of the Kenbak 1, the world's first personal computer, that went for $31,250.

Private

Nov. 24 1880

DOWN,
BECKENHAM, KENT.
RAILWAY STATION
ORPINGTON. S.E.R.

Dear Sir

I am sorry to have to inform you that I do not believe in the Bible as a divine revelation, & therefore not in Jesus Christ as the son of God.

Yours faithfully

Ch. Darwin

CHAPTER 10
Albert Einstein has spoken too

Albert Einstein's "God" Letter Sells for 3 Million 100 Dollars

Albert Einstein's so-called "God" letter, in which he expressed his opinion on God and religion shortly before his death has just sold for the (apparently) disappointing sum of $3,000,100.00 – just $100 more than the opening bid. The letter, written in 1954, was expected to fetch far more than this, although I would think the seller is more than happy with this figure. I know I would be.

This private letter expresses views never meant for public consumption by of one of the most prolific minds of modern times on the subjects of God, religion and tribalism.

Few people have had access to the thoughts and uncensored opinions of this brilliant mind as it relates to his personal views on God and religion. The personal nature of the letter and the timing of it in Albert Einstein's life adds to the implication of the certainty with which he wrote it. The sureness of his script and the methodical nature with which he chose his words lend to the documents weight. The ideas expressed are the culmination of a lifetime of work exploring the most principle questions of existence. If there were a guide for seekers of answers, this letter would be the introduction.

The auction is for the original, handwritten, in German, letter and envelope, sent from Princeton NJ, to Eric B. Gutkind, on January 3, 1954, a year before Einstein passed away, sent as response to Gutkind's book "Choose Life: The Biblical Call to Revolt".

I read a great deal in the last days of your book and thank you very much for sending it to me. What especially struck me about it was this. With regard to the factual attitude to life and to the human community we have a great deal in common.

The word God is for me nothing more than the expression and product of human weaknesses, the Bible a collection of honorable, but still primitive legends which are nevertheless pretty childish. No interpretation no matter how subtle can (for me) change this. These subtilized interpretations are highly manifold according to their nature and have almost nothing to do with the original text. For me the Jewish religion like all other religions is an incarnation of the most childish superstitions. And the Jewish people to whom I gladly belong and with whose mentality I have a deep affinity have no different quality for me than all other people. As far as my experience goes, they are also no better than other human groups, although they are protected from the worst cancers by a lack of power. Otherwise I cannot see anything 'chosen' about them.

In general I find it painful that you claim a privileged position and try to defend it by two walls of pride, an external one as a man and an internal one as a Jew. As a man you claim, so to speak, a dispensation from causality otherwise accepted, as a Jew the privilege of monotheism. But a limited causality is no longer a causality at all, as our wonderful Spinoza recognized with all incision, probably as the first one. And the animistic interpretations of the religions of nature are in principle not annulled by monopolization. With such walls we can only attain a certain self-deception, but our moral efforts are not furthered by them. On the contrary.

Now that I have quite openly stated our differences in intellectual convictions it is still clear to me that we are quite close to each other in essential things, i.e; in our evaluations of human behavior. What separates us are only intellectual 'props' and 'rationalization' in Freud's language. Therefore I think that we would understand each other quite well if we talked about concrete things.

With friendly thanks and best wishes,

Yours, A. Einstein

CHAPTER 11

Famous Atheists / Agnostics

Famous people who don't believe in God (Atheists or Agnostics):

Listed below, 45 famous people, from Ronald Reagan, Jr, son of President Ronald Reagan, to Dame Helen Mirren, made a Dame of the British Empire, by Queen Elizabeth II.

It's not uncommon to hear celebrities, athletes and stars thanking God for their success and winning awards, but the celebrities on this list are not going to be them. A lot of the stars on this list will shock you, yet some should come as no surprise at all. Whether they're atheists, agnostic or just Godless, everyone made their way onto this list by their own admissions.

For some confessions you'll have to watch the videos to find proof, and others we've found direct quotes elsewhere. If you're an atheist yourself you might enjoy the videos, but Christians and people of other faiths might find them very offensive, so for the most part we've left the decision to watch up to you.

Before we go any further, however, we want to make clear that the staff at Celebrity Tune spans many different religions, faiths and even the lack thereof, so we are offering absolutely no opinion on the matter of religion, just reporting the truth about some celebrities. You can also find our feature on the 27 most religious celebrities in the world today.

In the comments be sure to let us know what you think! Does this change how you view your favorite celebrities? Did we miss any?

RON REAGAN
Ron Reagan undertook a different philosophical and political path from his father at an early age. At 12, he told his parents that he would not be going to church anymore because he was an atheist.

KEANU REEVES
In 2005 Reeves said he was changing his thoughts on religion because a film was causing him to have fewer doubts about Heaven and Hell,

but also admitted to still being atheist. This was when the actor was promoting the film Constantine, which was of a religious nature.

JOHN LENNON

If you doubt Lennon's atheism look no further than his 1970 song "God."

God is a concept by which we can measure our pain…
I don't believe in magic, I don't believe in I-ching,
I don't believe in bible, I don't believe in tarot,
I don't believe in Hitler, I don't believe in Jesus,
I don't believe in Kennedy, I don't believe in Buddha,
I don't believe in mantra, I don't believe in Gita,
I don't believe in yoga, I don't believe in kings,
I don't believe in Elvis, I don't believe in Zimmerman,
I don't believe in Beatles…
I just believe in me, Yoko and me, and that's reality.

Also, in 1965 he said, "Christianity will go. It will vanish and shrink. I needn't argue with that; I'm right and I will be proved right. We're more popular than Jesus now; I don't know which will go first – rock and roll or Christianity."

MATT SMITH

The former Doctor Who, after reading The God Delusion by Richard Dawkins, said it "ignited my interest in a scientific, mathematical version of the world. No, I'm not religious. At all. I'm an atheist."

"Stupid, capricious and mean-minded" are just a few words used by Stephen Fry to describe God. Watch the clip to hear more.

SETH MACFARLANE

Raised Catholic, the writer/actor/director/comedian has turned religion into one big joke for his career, being quoted as saying

Stay away from the church. In the battle over science vs. religion, science offers credible evidence for all the serious claims it makes. The church says, 'Oh, it's right here in this book, see? The one written by people who thought the sun was magic?' I for one would like to see some proof that there is a God. And if you say 'a baby's smile' I'm going to kick you right in the stomach.

DARREN ARONOFSKY

Being one of the best directors in Hollywood undoubtedly means a lot to Aronofsky, which is why he probably calls his work his own god — "It's probably because I'm Godless. And so I've had to make my God, and my God is narrative filmmaking, which is — ultimately what my God becomes, which is what my mantra becomes, is the theme."

JAMES CAMERON

In his biography, the director of Titanic and Avatar, is quoted as saying, "I've sworn off agnosticism, which I now call cowardly atheism. I've come to the position that in the complete absence of any supporting data whatsoever for the persistence of the individual in some spiritual form, it is necessary to operate under the provisional conclusion that there is no afterlife and then be ready to amend that if I find out otherwise."

RICHARD BRANSON

The eccentric billionaire isn't the most obvious atheist on this list, but in his autobiography he gives us the proof we need when he wrote, "I do not believe in God, but as I sat there in the damaged [balloon] capsule, hopelessly vulnerable to the slightest shift in weather or mechanical fault, I could not believe my eyes." In the clip above, you'll notice he says he believes in evolution, not God.

LANCE ARMSTRONG

The one-time hero of the United States and legendary cyclist has expressed his doubts about a higher power many times, often citing his belief that he doesn't need religion to be a good person. Oddly, he never admitted to not needing steroids to be a good cyclist...

GEORGE CARLIN
R.I.P. George Carlin. Your brand of humor was brash, rude and unapologetic, especially when it came to religion. He had zero place for God in his life.

TREY PARKER & MATT STONE
In case you don't recognize the names, Parker and Stone are the creators of the TV show South Park, which has routinely mocked religion. They also brought The Book of Mormon to Broadway, with a song called "Hasa Diga Eebowai," which they translate to mean "F*** you, God." They call the musical their "atheist love letter to religion."

HARVEY FIERSTEIN
In the interview above, Fierstein admits to not believing in God, going so far to say the religions of others are "silly." Pretty sure that makes him an atheist.

MORGAN FREEMAN
The respected and successful actor Morgan Freeman adamantly states that he is not a man of God. He believes in science, and puts faith in science instead.

JODIE FOSTER
The Academy Award winning actress was asked point blank in 2007 if she was religious, and her answer left no doubt about her beliefs (or lack thereof) — "No, I'm an atheist. But I absolutely love religions and the rituals. Even though I don't believe in God. We celebrate pretty much every religion in our family with the kids. They love it, and when they say, 'Are we Jewish?' or 'Are we Catholic?' I say, 'Well, I'm not, but you can choose when you're 18. But isn't this fun that we do seders and the Advent calendar?'"

BILL GATES

Bill gates is one wealthy and philanthropic man, giving more to charity than any other human alive. He's also an atheist, saying in a Rolling Stone interview, "I agree with people like Richard Dawkins that mankind felt the need for creation myths. Before we really began to understand disease and the weather and things like that, we sought false explanations for them. Now science has filled in some of the realm – not all – that religion used to fill. But the mystery and the beauty of the world is overwhelmingly amazing, and there's no scientific explanation of how it came about. To say that it was generated by random numbers, that does seem, you know, sort of an uncharitable view [laughs]. I think it makes sense to believe in God, but exactly what decision in your life you make differently because of it, I don't know."

RICKY GERVAIS

If there is an heir to George Carlin regarding comedic sketches at the expense of religion, it's Ricky Gervais. Watch the clip above for proof. Need more proof? In a Daily Mirror interview the comedian said, "I'm basically a 'do unto others' type person. I don't have any religious feelings because I'm an atheist, but I live my life like there's a God. And if there was he'd probably love me."

ALAN CUMMING

Not only does Alan Cumming identify as an atheist, he is quoted as suggesting most Christians aren't either, that they just go through the motions in this quote — "I was made to go to church, but no, it wasn't a very religious thing. And I'm completely atheist. I don't hold any beliefs about God and stuff. And I can't do the church thing. Last year, I was here in New York, at a Christmas party, and everyone went to midnight Mass except me. I just listened to music while they were all out, supposedly communing with God, but they were just doing it because it's habit."

BILL MAHER

If you've never seen Real Time with Bill Maher, or seen his movie

Religulous, check out the clip from the ending of his movie, because he basically sums up his feelings right there. In his estimation, man and religion can't both survive.

DIANE KEATON

In 1987 Keaton identified as agnostic, but in a 2002 interview she called herself Christian, yet had once been an atheist. Woody Allen, a famous atheist in his own right, admitted that Keaton believes in God, but that "she also believes that the radio works because there are tiny people inside it."

KEIRA KNIGHTLY

In Interview Magazine the award winning actress and recent Oscar nominee said, "If only I wasn't an atheist, I could get away with anything. You'd just ask for forgiveness and then you'd be forgiven. It sounds much better than having to live with guilt."

Whoa! That's some serious shade toward religious people right there.

HUGH LAURIE

Most famous for playing the titular character in the hit TV show House (The character was also an atheist), Hugh Laurie is not a religious man, and definitely has some qualms with the Christian God, saying "I don't believe in God, but I have this idea that if there were a God, or destiny of some kind looking down on us, that if he saw you taking anything for granted he'd take it away. So he'll be like: 'You think this is going pretty well?' Then he'll go and send down some big disaster."

JULIANNE MOORE

No matter how blessed Christians might think the Oscar winner should be after all her success, Moore is definitely not a believer.

RAFAEL NADAL

You might be able to argue against the tennis hunk being called an atheist, but his quote in a 2010 issue of Sports Illustrated definitely hints that he's an atheist when he said, "It's hard to say, "I don't believe in God." I would love to know if God exists. But it's a very difficult thing for me to believe. I don't know. It's private and I don't want to speak about it, but I say, 'If God exists, you don't need [to cross yourself] or pray.' If God exists, he's intelligent enough to [do] the important things, the right things."

This, combined with his interview in Información, during which he said, "Almost every bad thing that happens in life comes from some form of radicalism, it only unleashes problems that should be fixed. You are entitled to have your likings, sympathies, beliefs, but you should always respect the opinions of others, never insult them. The same happens with religion. You can be religious, or atheist, christian, muslim... whatever, but I think the atrocities that people committed in the name of religion are too much. For me, religion is the main cause of immortality in history," definitely shows that the tennis legend at least isn't religious, even if he might believe in God.

JACK NICHOLSON

In an 1992 interview in Vanity Fair, Jack Nicholson said, "I don't believe in God now," but he added that "I can still work up an envy for someone who has a faith. I can see how that could be a deeply soothing experience."

JANEANE GAROFALO

In 2007 the actress described herself as an atheist on the Freethought Radio program, which is operated by the group Freedom From Religion.

BRAD PITT

Maybe the most famous actor in the world, Brad Pitt says religion "doesn't make sense."

JOAQUIN PHOENIX
Raised as part of the Children of God cult, Joaquin rebelled against all religion in adulthood, evidenced by his saying, "I don't believe in god. I don't believe in an afterlife. I don't believe in soul. I don't believe in anything. I think it's totally right for people to have their own beliefs if it makes them happy, but to me it's a pretty preposterous idea."

DANIEL RADCLIFFE
The magic wielding Harry Potter isn't religious! Even though he was raised by both Christian and Jewish parents, Daniel Radcliffe is definitely atheist. In the UK's gay magazine, Attitude, Radcliffe said, "I'm not religious, I'm an atheist, and a militant atheist when religion starts impacting on legislation. We need sex education in schools. Schools have to talk to kids from a young age about relationships, gay and straight. In Britain it's better – more of a conversation is being had."

GUILLERMO DEL TORO
Raised Catholic, del Toro not identifies as semi-agnostic, based on the following quote: "I'm semi-agnostic. I believe that there are so many things that are entirely unknowable that it's better to abandon yourself to the wisdom of the universe, or its indifference... I have constructed my own sort of personal religion... [that] doesn't depend on a guy in the sky that I pray to, but it does depend on trying to be as good a person as I can be."

LARRY KING
While the legendary TV personality is on record as stating, "Nearly every time, with one exception – if it comes to religious topics everything is already said. I am an agnostic, so I don't learn anything from them. But most of the time it's exciting." So, surely he isn't atheist, just agnostic, right?

Not so fast, when Barbara Walters asked him if he believed in God in 2005, he said, simply, "no."

EMMA THOMPSON

Emma Thompson may be Hollywood royalty, but she is definitely not a fan of religion. In fact, she's a stone-cold militant atheist, saying, "I'm an atheist; I suppose you can call me a sort of libertarian anarchist. I regard religion with fear and suspicion. It's not enough to say that I don't believe in God."

SEAN PENN

Okay, so Penn only identifies as agnostic, but his political involvement and views suggest his aversion to religion goes beyond that.

ANTONIO BANDERAS

Antonio Banderas only claims agnosticism, but he's fine if his kids are atheists.

UMA THURMAN

The Kill Bill and Pulp Fiction star said, "When asked if I consider myself Buddhist, the answer is, 'Not really'. But it's more my religion than any other because I was brought up with it in an intellectual and spiritual environment. I don't practice or preach it, however. But Buddhism has had a major effect on who I am and how I think about the world. What I have learned is that I like all religions, but only parts of them." So, if Buddhism isn't her religion, that really means she doesn't have one at all.

KEVIN BACON

In Times of London Kevin Bacon said he doesn't believe in God, despite being raised Catholic. He joins a long list of celebrities giving up religion after having success.

JAVIER BARDEM

Born in Spain, Bardem has a good understanding of religion, having been raised Catholic, but now he says, "I don't understand religion when it gets to the point where the beyond commands the present, because then the present doesn't have any sense. . . . Myself, I really need to know and face mortality: I am this, I am me, I am now."

NATALIE DORMER

The British actress most famous for playing Margaery Tyrell in HBO's Game of Thrones in 2007 said, "I say I'm an atheist but I wouldn't mind being visited by a ghost." Well, there you go.

PAUL GIAMATTI

Appearing in The Guardian, Giamatti is quoted as having said, "I consider myself an atheist. My wife is Jewish. And I'm fine with my son being raised as a Jew. He's learning Hebrew and is really into it. I will talk to my own son about my atheism when the time is right. But there's a great tradition of Jewish atheism, there are no better atheists in the world than the Jews."

Not only is he not religious, but he appears to imply that the Jewish people are better than folks of other religions.

SETH GREEN

Whoa! Seth Green is what one might call a militant atheist, not only does he deny religion, but even insults those who believe in it — "God is, to me, pretty much a myth created over time to deny the idea that we're all responsible for our own actions."

KATHY GRIFFIN

Holy sh*t. Yes, she said it. Just let that sink in.

IRA GLASS

Ira Glass is one of the most famous radio personalities in the world, hosting "This American Life" on Public Radio International, syndicated by NPR all over America. He's not exactly rude to people of faith, but he does call religion "arbitrary." Not the nicest way to describe something very important to millions of Americans.

SIR IAN MCKELLEN

Openly gay actor Sir Ian McKellen is an avowed atheist, having said, "I was brought up a Christian, low church, and I like the community of churchgoing. That's rather been replaced for me by the community of people I work with. I like a sense of family, of people working together. But I'm an atheist. So God, if She exists, isn't really a part of my life." But he takes it one step further, ripping up Bibles in hotel rooms where he stays.

DAME HELEN MIRREN

Regal and an Oscar winner, Dame Helen Mirren describes herself as "a Christian who doesn't believe in God. I can't help being Christian because I was brought up in Britain and the morality of Christianity is part of the fabric of this country.

But I don't believe in God. But I do believe in treating other people as you'd want to be treated and being empathetic."

PATTON OSWALT

In the above video you can see what the comedian says about religion. He definitely says he's an atheist, but he also says so much more. (NSFW)

SARAH SILVERMAN

The Jewish-American comedian often uses religion as a punchline, saying she's glad that the Jews killed Jesus, and she'd do it again in some of her sketches. You can see some of it in the above NSFW clip.

From www.wably.com

CHAPTER 12
The Forged Origins of the New Testament

In the fourth century, the Roman Emperor Constantine united all religious factions under one composite deity, and ordered the compilation of new and old writings into a uniform collection that became the New Testament.

What the Church doesn't want you to know

It has often been emphasised that Christianity is unlike any other religion, for it stands or falls by certain events which are alleged to have occurred during a short period of time some 20 centuries ago. Those stories are presented in the New Testament, and as new evidence is revealed it will become clear that they do not represent historical realities. The Church agrees, saying: "Our documentary sources of knowledge about the origins of Christianity and its earliest development are chiefly the New Testament Scriptures, the authenticity of which we must, to a great extent, take for granted." (Catholic Encyclopedia, Farley ed., vol. iii, p. 712).

The Church makes extraordinary admissions about its New Testament. For example, when discussing the origin of those writings, "the most distinguished body of academic opinion ever assembled" (Catholic Encyclopedias, Preface) admits that the Gospels "do not go back to the first century of the Christian era" (Catholic Encyclopedia, Farley ed., vol. vi, p. 137, pp. 655-6). This statement conflicts with priesthood assertions that the earliest Gospels were progressively written during the decades following the death of the Gospel Jesus Christ. In a remarkable aside, the Church further admits that "the earliest of the extant manuscripts [of the New Testament], it is true, do not date back beyond the middle of the fourth century AD" (Catholic Encyclopedia, op. cit., pp. 656-7). That is some 350 years after the time the Church claims that a Jesus Christ walked the sands of Palestine, and here the true story of Christian origins slips into one of the biggest black holes in history. There is, however, a reason why there were no New Testaments until the fourth century: they were not written until then, and here we find evidence of the greatest misrepresentation of all time.

It was British-born Flavius Constantinus (Constantine, originally Custennyn or Custennin) (272-337) who authorised the compilation of the writings now called the New Testament. After the death of his father in 306, Constantine became King of Britain, Gaul and Spain, and then, after a series of victorious battles, Emperor of the Roman Empire. Christian historians give little or no hint of the turmoil of the times and suspend Constantine in the air, free of all human events happening around him. In truth, one of Constantine's main problems was the uncontrollable disorder amongst presbyters and their belief in numerous gods.

The majority of modern-day Christian writers suppress the truth about the development of their religion and conceal Constantine's efforts to curb the disreputable character of the presbyters who are now called "Church Fathers" (Catholic Encyclopedia, Farley ed., vol. xiv, pp. 370-1). They were "maddened", he said (Life of Constantine, attributed to Eusebius Pamphilius of Caesarea, c. 335, vol. iii, p. 171 ; The Nicene and Post-Nicene Fathers, cited as N&PNF, attributed to St Ambrose, Rev. Prof. Roberts, DD, and Principal James Donaldson, LLD, editors, 1891, vol. iv, p. 467). The "peculiar type of oratory" expounded by them was a challenge to a settled religious order (The Dictionary of Classical Mythology, Religion, Literature and Art, Oskar Seyffert, Gramercy, New York, 1995, pp. 544-5). Ancient records reveal the true nature of the presbyters, and the low regard in which they were held has been subtly suppressed by modern Church historians. In reality, they were: "...the most rustic fellows, teaching strange paradoxes. They openly declared that none but the ignorant was fit to hear their discourses ... they never appeared in the circles of the wiser and better sort, but always took care to intrude themselves among the ignorant and uncultured, rambling around to play tricks at fairs and markets ... they lard their lean books with the fat of old fables ... and still the less do they understand ... and they write nonsense on vellum ... and still be doing, never done." (Contra Celsum ["Against Celsus"], Origen of Alexandria, c. 251 , Bk I, p. lxvii, Bk III, p. xliv, passim)

Clusters of presbyters had developed "many gods and many lords" (1 Cor. 8:5) and numerous religious sects existed, each with differing doctrines (Gal. 1 :6). Presbyterial groups clashed over attributes of their various gods and "altar was set against altar" in competing for an audience (Optatus of Milevis, 1 :1 5, 19, early fourth century). From Constantine's point of view, there were several factions that needed satisfying, and he set out to develop an all-embracing religion during a period of irreverent confusion. In an age of crass ignorance, with nine-tenths of the peoples of Europe illiterate, stabilizing religious splinter groups was only one of Constantine's problems. The smooth generalization, which so many historians are content to repeat, that Constantine "embraced the Christian religion" and subsequently granted "official toleration", is "contrary to historical fact" and should be erased from our literature forever (Catholic Encyclopedia, Pecci ed., vol. iii, p. 299, passim). Simply put, there was no Christian religion at Constantine's time, and the Church acknowledges that the tale of his "conversion" and "baptism" are "entirely legendary" (Catholic Encyclopedia, Farley ed., vol. xiv, pp. 370-1).

Constantine "never acquired a solid theological knowledge" and "depended heavily on his advisers in religious questions" (Catholic Encyclopedia, New Edition, vol. xii, p. 576, passim). According to Eusebeius (260-339), Constantine noted that among the presbyterian factions "strife had grown so serious, vigorous action was necessary to establish a more religious state", but he could not bring about a settlement between rival god factions (Life of Constantine, op. cit., pp. 26-8). His advisers warned him that the presbyters' religions were "destitute of foundation" and needed official stabilization (ibid.).

Constantine saw in this confused system of fragmented dogmas the opportunity to create a new and combined State religion, neutral in concept, and to protect it by law. When he conquered the East in 324 he sent his Spanish religious adviser, Osius of Cordoba, to Alexandria with letters to several bishops exhorting them to make peace among themselves. The mission failed and Constantine, probably at the suggestion of Osius, then issued a decree commanding all presbyters and their subordinates "be mounted on asses, mules and horses belonging to the public, and travel to the city of Nicaea" in the Roman province of Bithynia in Asia Minor. They were instructed to bring with them the testimonies they orated to the rabble, "bound in leather" for protection during the long journey, and surrender them to Constantine upon arrival in Nicaea (The Catholic Dictionary, Addis and Arnold, 1917, "Council of Nicaea" entry). Their writings totalled "in all, two thousand two hundred and thirty-one scrolls and legendary tales of gods and saviours, together with a record of the doctrines orated by them" (Life of Constantine, op. cit., vol. ii, p. 73; N&PNF, op. cit., vol. i, p. 518).

The First Council of Nicaea and the "missing records"

Thus, the first ecclesiastical gathering in history was summoned and is today known as the Council of Nicaea. It was a bizarre event that provided many details of early clerical thinking and presents a clear picture of the intellectual climate prevailing at the time. It was at this gathering that Christianity was born, and the ramifications of decisions made at the time are difficult to calculate. About four years prior to chairing the Council, Constantine had been initiated into the religious order of Sol Invictus, one of the two thriving cults that regarded the Sun as the one and only Supreme God (the other was Mithraism). Because of his Sun worship, he instructed Eusebius to convene the first of three sittings on the summer solstice, 21 June 325 (Catholic Encyclopedia, New Edition, vol. i, p. 792), and it was "held in a hall in Osius's palace" {Ecclesiastical History, Bishop Louis Dupin, Paris, 1686, vol. i, p. 598). In an account of the proceedings of the conclave of presbyters gathered at Nicaea, Sabinius, Bishop of Hereclea, who was in attendance, said, "Excepting Constantine himself and Eusebius Pamphilius, they were a set of illiterate, simple creatures who understood nothing" (Secrets of the Christian Fathers, Bishop J. W. Sergerus, 1685, 1897 reprint).

This is another luminous confession of the ignorance and uncritical credulity of early churchmen. Dr Richard Watson (1737-1816), a disillusioned Christian historian and one-time Bishop of Llandaff in Wales (1782), referred to them as "a set of gibbering idiots" {An Apology for Christianity, 1776, 1796 reprint; also, Theological Tracts, Dr Richard Watson, "On Councils" entry, vol. 2, London, 1786, revised reprint 1791). From his extensive research into Church councils, Dr Watson concluded that "the clergy at the Council of Nicaea were all under the power of the devil, and the convention was composed of the lowest rabble and patronised the vilest abominations" {An Apology for Christianity, op. cit.). It was that infantile body of men who were responsible for the commencement of a new religion and the theological creation of Jesus Christ.

The Church admits that vital elements of the proceedings at Nicaea are "strangely absent from the canons" {Catholic Encyclopedia, Farley ed., vol. iii, p. 160). We shall see shortly what happened to them. However, according to records that endured, Eusebius "occupied the first seat on the right of the emperor and delivered the inaugural address on the emperor's behalf" {Catholic Encyclopedia, Farley ed., vol. v, pp. 619-620). There were no British presbyters at the council but many Greek delegates. "Seventy Eastern bishops" represented Asiatic factions, and small numbers came from other areas {Ecclesiastical History, ibid.). Caecilian of Carthage travelled from Africa, Paphnutius of Thebes from Egypt, Nicasius of Die (Dijon) from Gaul, and Donnus of Stridon made the journey from Pannonia.

It was at that puerile assembly, and with so many cults represented, that a total of 318 "bishops, priests, deacons, subdeacons, acolytes and exorcists" gathered to debate and decide upon a unified belief system that encompassed only one god (An Apology for Christianity, op. cit.). By this time, a huge assortment of "wild texts" (Catholic Encyclopedia, New Edition, "Gospel and Gospels") circulated amongst presbyters and they supported a great variety of Eastern and Western gods and goddesses: Jove, Jupiter, Salenus, Baal, Thor, Gade, Apollo, Juno, Aries, Taurus, Minerva, Rhets, Mithra, Theo, Fragapatti, Atys, Durga, Indra, Neptune, Vulcan, Kriste, Agni, Croesus, Pelides, Huit, Hermes, Thulis, Thammus, Eguptus, Iao, Aph, Saturn, Gitchens, Minos, Maximo, Heclaand Phernes (God's Book of Eskra, anon., ch. xlviii, paragraph 36).

Up until the First Council of Nicaea, the Roman aristocracy primarily worshipped two Greek gods-Apollo and Zeus-but the great bulk of common people idolised either Julius Caesar or Mithras (the Romanised version of the Persian deity Mithra). Caesar was deified by the Roman Senate after his death (15 March 44 BC) and subsequently venerated as "the Divine Julius". The word "Saviour" was affixed to his name, its literal meaning being "one who sows the seed", i.e., he was a phallic god. Julius Caesar was hailed as "God made manifest and universal Saviour of human life", and his successor Augustus was called the "ancestral God and Saviour of the whole human race" (Man and his Gods, Homer Smith, Little, Brown & Co., Boston, 1952). Emperor Nero (54-68), whose original name was Lucius Domitius

Ahenobarbus (37-68), was immortalised on his coins as the "Saviour of mankind" (ibid.). The Divine Julius as Roman Saviour and "Father of the Empire" was considered "God" among the Roman rabble for more than 300 years. He was the deity in some Western presbyters' texts, but was not recognised in Eastern or Oriental writings.

Constantine's intention at Nicaea was to create an entirely new god for his empire who would unite all religious factions under one deity. Presbyters were asked to debate and decide who their new god would be. Delegates argued among themselves, expressing personal motives for inclusion of particular writings that promoted the finer traits of their own special deity. Throughout the meeting, howling factions were immersed in heated debates, and the names of 53 gods were tabled for discussion. "As yet, no God had been selected by the council, and so they balloted in order to determine that matter... For one year and five months the balloting lasted..." (God's Book of Eskra, Prof. S. L. MacGuire's translation, Salisbury, 1922, chapter xlviii, paragraphs 36, 41).

At the end of that time, Constantine returned to the gathering to discover that the presbyters had not agreed on a new deity but had balloted down to a shortlist of five prospects: Caesar, Krishna, Mithra, Horus and Zeus (Historia Ecclesiastica, Eusebius, c. 325). Constantine was the ruling spirit at Nicaea and he ultimately decided upon a new god for them. To involve British factions, he ruled that the name of the great Druid god, Hesus, be joined with the Eastern Saviour-god, Krishna (Krishna is Sanskrit for Christ), and thus Hesus Krishna would be the official name of the new Roman god. A vote was taken and it was with a majority show of hands (1 61 votes to 1 57) that both divinities became one God. Following longstanding heathen custom, Constantine used the official gathering and the Roman apotheosis decree to legally deify two deities as one, and did so by democratic consent. A new god was proclaimed and "officially" ratified by Constantine (Acta Concilii Nicaeni, 1618). That purely political act of deification effectively and legally placed Hesus and Krishna among the Roman gods as one individual composite. That abstraction lent Earthly existence to amalgamated doctrines for the Empire's new religion; and because there was no letter "J" in alphabets until around the ninth century, the name subsequently evolved into "Jesus Christ".

How the Gospels were created

Constantine then instructed Eusebius to organize the compilation of a uniform collection of new writings developed from primary aspects of the religious texts submitted at the council. His instructions were: "Search ye these books, and whatever is good in them, that retain; but whatsoever is evil, that cast away. What is good in one book, unite ye with that which is good in another book. And whatsoever is thus brought together shall be called The Book of Books. And it shall be the doctrine of my people, which I will recommend unto all nations, that there shall be no more war for religions' sake." (God's Book of Eskra, op. cit., chapter xlviii, paragraph 31)

"Make them to astonish" said Constantine, and "the books were written accordingly" (Life of Constantine, vol. iv, pp. 36-39). Eusebius amalgamated the "legendary tales of all the religious doctrines of the world together as one", using the standard god-myths from the presbyters' manuscripts as his exemplars. Merging the supernatural "god" stories of Mithra and Krishna with British Culdean beliefs effectively joined the orations of Eastern and Western presbyters together "to form a new universal belief" (ibid.). Constantine believed that the amalgamated collection of myths would unite variant and opposing religious factions under one representative story. Eusebius then arranged for scribes to produce "fifty sumptuous copies ... to be written on parchment in a legible manner, and in a convenient portable form, by professional scribes thoroughly accomplished in their art" (ibid.). "These orders," said Eusebius, "were followed by the immediate execution of the work itself ... we sent him [Constantine] magnificently and elaborately bound volumes of three-fold and four-fold forms" (Life of Constantine, vol. iv, p. 36). They were the "New Testimonies", and this is the first mention (c. 331) of the New Testament in the historical record.

With his instructions fulfilled, Constantine then decreed that the New Testimonies would thereafter be called the "word of the Roman Saviour God" (Life of Constantine, vol. iii, p. 29) and official to all presbyters sermonising in the Roman Empire. He then ordered earlier presbyterial manuscripts and the records of the council "burnt" and declared that "any man found concealing writings should be stricken off from his shoulders" (beheaded) (ibid.). As the record shows, presbyterial writings previous to the Council of Nicaea no longer exist, except for some fragments that have survived. Some council records also survived, and they provide alarming ramifications for the Church. Some old documents say that the First Council of Nicaea ended in mid-November 326, while others say the struggle to establish a god was so fierce that it extended "for four years and seven months" from its beginning in June 325 (Secrets of the Christian Fathers, op. cit.). Regardless of when it ended, the savagery and violence it encompassed were concealed under the glossy title "Great and Holy Synod", assigned to the assembly by the Church in the 18th century. Earlier Churchmen, however, expressed a different opinion.

The Second Council of Nicaea in 786-87 denounced the First Council of Nicaea as "a synod of fools and madmen" and sought to annul "decisions passed by men with troubled brains" (History of the Christian Church, H. H. Milman, DD, 1871). If one chooses to read the records of the Second Nicaean Council and notes references to "affrighted bishops" and the "soldiery" needed to "quell proceedings", the "fools and madmen" declaration is surely an example of the pot calling the kettle black.

Constantine died in 337 and his outgrowth of many now-called pagan beliefs into a new religious system brought many converts. Later Church writers made him "the great champion of Christianity" which he gave "legal status as the religion of the Roman Empire" (Encyclopedia of the Roman Empire, Matthew Bunson, Facts on File, New York, 1994, p. 86). Historical records reveal this to be incorrect, for it was "self-interest" that led him to create Christianity (A Smaller Classical Dictionary, J. M. Dent, London, 1 910, p. 161). Yet it wasn't called "Christianity" until the 1 5th century (How The Great Pan Died, Professor Edmond S. Bordeaux [Vatican archivist], Mille Meditations, USA, MCMLXVIII, pp. 45-7).

Over the ensuing centuries, Constantine's New Testimonies were expanded upon, "interpolations" were added and other writings included (Catholic Encyclopedia, Farley ed., vol. vi, pp. 135-137; also, Pecci ed., vol. ii, pp. 121-122). For example, in 397 John "golden-mouthed" Chrysostom restructured the writings of Apollonius of Tyana, a first-century wandering sage, and made them part of the New Testimonies (Secrets of the Christian Fathers, op. cit.). The Latinised name for Apollonius is Paulus (A Latin-English Dictionary, J. T. White and J. E. Riddle, Ginn & Heath, Boston, 1880), and the Church today calls those writings the Epistles of Paul. Apollonius's personal attendant, Damis, an Assyrian scribe, is Demis in the New Testament (2 Tim. 4:10).

The Church hierarchy knows the truth about the origin of its Epistles, for Cardinal Bembo (d. 1547), secretary to Pope Leo X (d. 1521), advised his associate, Cardinal Sadoleto, to disregard them, saying "put away these trifles, for such absurdities do not become a man of dignity; they were introduced on the scene later by a sly voice from heaven" (Cardinal Bembo: His Letters and Comments on Pope Leo X, A. L. Collins, London, 1842 reprint).

The Church admits that the Epistles of Paul are forgeries, saying, "Even the genuine Epistles were greatly interpolated to lend weight to the personal views of their authors" (Catholic Encyclopedia, Farley ed., vol. vii, p. 645). Likewise, St Jerome (d. 420) declared that the Acts of the Apostles, the fifth book of the New Testament, was also "falsely written" ("The Letters of Jerome", Library of the Fathers, Oxford Movement, 1833-45, vol. v, p. 445).

The shock discovery of an ancient Bible

The New Testament subsequently evolved into a fulsome piece of priesthood propaganda, and the Church claimed it recorded the intervention of a divine Jesus Christ into Earthly affairs. However, a spectacular discovery in a remote Egyptian monastery revealed to the world the extent of later falsifications of the Christian texts, themselves only an "assemblage of legendary tales" (Encyclopedie , Diderot, 1759). On 4 February 1859, 346 leaves of an ancient codex were discovered in the furnace room at St Catherine's monastery at Mt Sinai, and its contents sent shockwaves through the Christian world. Along with other old codices, it was scheduled to be burned in the kilns to provide winter warmth for the inhabitants of the monastery. Written in Greek on donkey skins, it carried both the Old and New

Testaments, and later in time archaeologists dated its composition to around the year 380. It was discovered by Dr Constantin von Tischendorf (1 81 5-1874), a brilliant and pious German biblical scholar, and he called it the Sinaiticus, the Sinai Bible. Tischendorf was a professor of theology who devoted his entire life to the study of New Testament origins, and his desire to read all the ancient Christian texts led him on the long, camel-mounted journey to St Catherine's Monastery.

During his lifetime, Tischendorf had access to other ancient Bibles unavailable to the public, such as the Alexandrian (or Alexandrinus) Bible, believed to be the second oldest Bible in the world. It was so named because in 1627 it was taken from Alexandria to Britain and gifted to King Charles I (1600-49). Today it is displayed alongside the world's oldest known Bible, the Sinaiticus, in the British Library in London. During his research, Tischendorf had access to the Vaticanus, the Vatican Bible, believed to be the third oldest in the world and dated to the mid-sixth century (The Various Versions of the Bible, Dr Constantin von Tischendorf, 1874, available in the British Library). It was locked away in the Vatican's inner library. Tischendorf asked if he could extract handwritten notes, but his request was declined. However, when his guard took refreshment breaks, Tischendorf wrote comparative narratives on the palm of his hand and sometimes on his fingernails ("Are Our Gospels Genuine or Not?", Dr Constantin von Tischendorf, lecture, 1869, available in the British Library).

Today, there are several other Bibles written in various languages during the fifth and sixth centuries, examples being the Syriacus, the Cantabrigiensis (Bezae), the Sarravianus and the Marchaiianus.

A shudder of apprehension echoed through Christendom in the last quarter of the 19th century when English-language versions of the Sinai Bible were published. Recorded within these pages is information that disputes Christianity's claim of historicity. Christians were provided with irrefutable evidence of wilful falsifications in all modern New Testaments. So different was the Sinai Bible's New Testament from versions then being published that the Church angrily tried to annul the dramatic new evidence that challenged its very existence. In a series of articles published in the London Quarterly Review in 1883,

John W. Burgon, Dean of Chichester, used every rhetorical device at his disposal to attack the Sinaiticus' earlier and opposing story of Jesus Christ, saying that "...without a particle of hesitation, the Sinaiticus is scandalously corrupt ... exhibiting the most shamefully mutilated texts which are anywhere to be met with; they have become, by whatever process, the depositories of the largest amount of fabricated readings, ancient blunders and intentional perversions of the truth which are discoverable in any known copies of the word of God". Dean Burgon's concerns mirror opposing aspects of Gospel stories then current, having by now evolved to a new stage through centuries of tampering with the fabric of an already unhistorical document.

The revelations of ultraviolet light testing

In 1933, the British Museum in London purchased the Sinai Bible from the Soviet government for £100,000, of which £65,000 was gifted by public subscription. Prior to the acquisition, this Bible was displayed in the Imperial Library in St Petersburg, Russia, and "few scholars had set eyes on it" (The Daily Telegraph and Morning Post, 1 1 January 1 938, p. 3). When it went on display in 1 933 as "the oldest Bible in the world" (ibid.), it became the centre of a pilgrimage unequalled in the history of the British Museum.

Before I summarise its conflictions, it should be noted that this old codex is by no means a reliable guide to New Testament study as it contains superabundant errors and serious re-editing. These anomalies were exposed as a result of the months of ultraviolet-light tests carried out at the British Museum in the mid-1930s. The findings revealed replacements of numerous passages by at least nine different editors. Photographs taken during testing revealed that ink pigments had been retained deep in the pores of the skin. The original words were readable under ultraviolet light. Anybody wishing to read the results of the tests should refer to the book written by the researchers who did the analysis: the Keepers of the Department of Manuscripts at the British Museum (Scribes and Correctors of the Codex Sinaiticus, H. J. M. Milne and T. C. Skeat, British Museum, London, 1938).

Forgery in the Gospels

When the New Testament in the Sinai Bible is compared with a modern-day New Testament, a staggering 14,800 editorial alterations can be identified. These amendments can be recognised by a simple comparative exercise that anybody can and should do. Serious study of Christian origins must emanate from the Sinai Bible's version of the New Testament, not modern editions.

Of importance is the fact that the Sinaiticus carries three Gospels since rejected: the Shepherd of Hermas (written by two resurrected ghosts, Charinus and Lenthius), the Missive of Barnabas and the Odes of Solomon. Space excludes elaboration on these bizarre writings and also discussion on dilemmas associated with translation variations.

Modern Bibles are five removes in translation from early editions, and disputes rage between translators over variant interpretations of more than 5,000 ancient words. However, it is what is not written in that old Bible that embarrasses the Church, and this article discusses only a few of those omissions. One glaring example is subtly revealed in the Encyclopaedia Biblica (Adam & Charles Black, London, 1899, vol. iii, p. 3344), where the Church divulges its knowledge about exclusions in old Bibles, saying: "The remark has long ago and often been made that, like Paul, even the earliest Gospels knew nothing of the miraculous birth of our Saviour". That is because there never was a virgin birth.

It is apparent that when Eusebius assembled scribes to write the New Testimonies, he first produced a single document that provided an exemplar or master version. Today it is called the Gospel of Mark, and the Church admits that it was "the first Gospel written" (Catholic Encyclopedia, Farley ed., vol. vi, p. 657), even though it appears second in the New Testament today. The scribes of the Gospels of Matthew and Luke were dependent upon the Mark writing as the source and framework for the compilation of their works. The Gospel of John is independent of those writings, and the late-15th-century theory that it was written later to support the earlier writings is the truth (The Crucifixion of Truth, Tony Bushby, Joshua Books, 2004, pp. 33-40).

Thus, the Gospel of Mark in the Sinai Bible carries the "first" story of Jesus Christ in history, one completely different to what is in modern Bibles. It starts with Jesus "at about the age of thirty" (Mark 1 :9), and doesn't know of Mary, a virgin birth or mass murders of baby boys by Herod. Words describing Jesus Christ as "the son of God" do not appear in the opening narrative as they do in today's editions (Mark 1 :1), and the modern-day family tree tracing a "messianic bloodline" back to King David is non-existent in all ancient Bibles, as are the now-called "messianic prophecies" (51 in total). The Sinai Bible carries a conflicting version of events surrounding the "raising of Lazarus", and reveals an extraordinary omission that later became the central doctrine of the Christian faith: the resurrection appearances of Jesus Christ and his ascension into Heaven. No supernatural appearance of a resurrected Jesus Christ is recorded in any ancient Gospels of Mark, but a description of over 500 words now appears in modern Bibles (Mark 16:9-20).

Despite a multitude of long-drawn-out self-justifications by Church apologists, there is no unanimity of Christian opinion regarding the non-existence of "resurrection" appearances in ancient Gospel accounts of the story. Not only are those narratives missing in the Sinai Bible, but they are absent in the Alexandrian Bible, the Vatican Bible, the Bezae Bible and an ancient Latin manuscript of Mark, code-named "K" by analysts. They are also lacking in the oldest Armenian version of the New Testament, in sixth-century manuscripts of the Ethiopic version and ninth-century Anglo-Saxon Bibles. However, some 12th-century Gospels have the now-known resurrection verses written within asterisks marks used by scribes to indicate spurious passages in a literary document.

The Church claims that "the resurrection is the fundamental argument for our Christian belief" (Catholic Encyclopedia, Farley ed., vol. xii, p. 792), yet no supernatural appearance of a resurrected Jesus Christ is recorded in any of the earliest Gospels of Mark available. A resurrection and ascension of Jesus Christ is the sine qua non ("without which, nothing") of Christianity (Catholic Encyclopedia, Farley ed., vol. xii, p. 792), confirmed by words attributed to Paul: "If Christ has not been raised, your faith is in vain" (1 Cor. 5:17). The resurrection verses in today's Gospels of Mark are universally acknowledged as forgeries and the Church agrees, saying "the conclusion of Mark is admittedly not genuine ... almost the entire section is a later compilation" (Encyclopaedia Biblica, vol. ii, p. 1880, vol. iii, pp. 1767, 1781; also, Catholic Encyclopedia, vol. iii, under the heading "The Evidence of its Spuriousness"; Catholic Encyclopedia, Farley ed., vol. iii, pp. 274-9 under heading "Canons"). Undaunted, however, the Church accepted the forgery into its dogma and made it the basis of Christianity.

The trend of fictitious resurrection narratives continues. The final chapter of the Gospel of John (21) is a sixth-century forgery, one entirely devoted to describing Jesus' resurrection to his disciples. The Church admits: "The sole conclusion that can be deduced from this is that the 21st chapter was afterwards added and is therefore to be regarded as an appendix to the Gospel" (Catholic Encyclopedia, Farley ed., vol. viii, pp. 441-442; New Catholic Encyclopedia (NCE), "Gospel of John", p. 1080; also NCE, vol. xii, p. 407).

"The Great Insertion" and "The Great Omission"

Modern-day versions of the Gospel of Luke have a staggering 10,000 more words than the same Gospel in the Sinai Bible. Six of those words say of Jesus "and was carried up into heaven", but this narrative does not appear in any of the oldest Gospels of Luke available today ("Three Early Doctrinal Modifications of the Text of the Gospels", F. C. Conybeare, The Hibbert Journal, London, vol. 1 , no. 1 , Oct 1 902, pp. 96-1 1 3). Ancient versions do not verify modern-day accounts of an ascension of Jesus Christ, and this falsification clearly indicates an intention to deceive.

Today, the Gospel of Luke is the longest of the canonical Gospels because it now includes "The Great Insertion", an extraordinary 15th-century addition totalling around 8,500 words (Luke 9:51 -18:1 4). The insertion of these forgeries into that Gospel bewilders modern Christian analysts, and of them the Church said: "The character of these passages makes it dangerous to draw inferences" (Catholic Encyclopedia, Pecci ed., vol. ii, p. 407).

Just as remarkable, the oldest Gospels of Luke omit all verses from 6:45 to 8:26, known in priesthood circles as "The Great Omission", a total of 1 ,547 words. In today's versions, that hole has been "plugged up" with passages plagiarised from other Gospels. Dr Tischendorf found that three paragraphs in newer versions of the Gospel of Luke's version of the Last Supper appeared in the 15th century, but the Church still passes its Gospels off as the unadulterated "word of God" ("Are Our Gospels Genuine or Not?", op. cit.)

The "Expurgatory Index"

As was the case with the New Testament, so also were damaging writings of early "Church Fathers" modified in centuries of copying, and many of their records were intentionally rewritten or suppressed.

Adopting the decrees of the Council of Trent (1545-63), the Church subsequently extended the process of erasure and ordered the preparation of a special list of specific information to be expunged from early Christian writings (Delineation of Roman Catholicism, Rev. Charles Elliott, DD, G. Lane & P. P. Sandford, New York, 1842, p. 89; also, The Vatican Censors, Professor Peter Elmsley, Oxford, p. 327, pub. date n/a).

In 1562, the Vatican established a special censoring office called Index Expurgatorius. Its purpose was to prohibit publication of "erroneous passages of the early Church Fathers" that carried statements opposing modern-day doctrine.

When Vatican archivists came across "genuine copies of the Fathers, they corrected them according to the Expurgatory Index" (Index Expurgatorius Vaticanus, R. Gibbings, ed., Dublin, 1837; The Literary Policy of the Church of Rome, Joseph Mendham, J. Duncan, London, 1830, 2nd ed., 1840; The Vatican Censors, op. cit., p. 328). This Church record provides researchers with "grave doubts about the value of all patristic writings released to the public" (The Propaganda Press of Rome, Sir James W. L. Claxton, Whitehaven Books, London, 1942, p. 182).

Important for our story is the fact that the Encyclopaedia Biblica reveals that around 1,200 years of Christian history are unknown: "Unfortunately, only few of the records [of the Church] prior to the year 1198 have been released". It was not by chance that, in that same year (1198), Pope Innocent 111(1198-1216) suppressed all records of earlier Church history by establishing the Secret Archives (Catholic Encyclopedia, Farley ed., voi. xv, p. 287). Some seven-and-a-half centuries later, and after spending some years in those Archives, Professor Edmond S. Bordeaux wrote How The Great Pan Died. In a chapter titled "The Whole of Church History is Nothing but a Retroactive Fabrication", he said this (in part): "The Church ante-dated all her late works, some newly made, some revised and some counterfeited, which contained the final expression of her history ... her technique was to make it appear that much later works written by Church writers were composed a long time earlier, so that they might become evidence of the first, second or third centuries." (i How The Great Pan Died, op. cit., p. 46)

Supporting Professor Bordeaux's findings is the fact that, in 1587, Pope Sixtus V (1585-90) established an official Vatican publishing division and said in his own words, "Church history will be now be established ... we shall seek to print our own account" Encyclopedie, Diderot, 1759). Vatican records also reveal that Sixtus V spent 18 months of his life as pope personally writing a new Bible and then introduced into Catholicism a "New Learning" (Catholic Encyclopedia, Farley ed., vol. v, p. 442, vol. xv, p. 376). The evidence that the Church wrote its own history is found in Diderot's Encyclopedie, and it reveals the reason why Pope Clement XIII (1758-69) ordered all volumes to be destroyed immediately after publication in 1759.

Gospel authors exposed as imposters

There is something else involved in this scenario and it is recorded in the Catholic Encyclopedia. An appreciation of the clerical mindset arises when the Church itself admits that it does not know who wrote its Gospels and Epistles, confessing that all 27 New Testament writings began life anonymously: "It thus appears that the present titles of the Gospels are not traceable to the evangelists themselves ... they [the New Testament collection] are supplied with titles which, however ancient, do not go back to the respective authors of those writings." (Catholic Encyclopedia, Farley ed., vol. vi, pp. 655-6)

The Church maintains that "the titles of our Gospels were not intended to indicate authorship", adding that "the headings ... were affixed to them" (Catholic Encyclopedia, Farley ed., vol. i, p. 117, vol. vi, pp. 655, 656). Therefore they are not Gospels written "according to Matthew, Mark, Luke or John", as publicly stated. The full force of this confession reveals that there are no genuine apostolic Gospels, and that the Church's shadowy writings today embody the very ground and pillar of Christian foundations and faith. The consequences are fatal to the pretence of Divine origin of the entire New Testament and expose Christian texts as having no special authority. For centuries, fabricated Gospels bore Church certification of authenticity now confessed to be false, and this provides evidence that Christian writings are wholly fallacious.

After years of dedicated New Testament research, Dr Tischendorf expressed dismay at the differences between the oldest and newest Gospels, and had trouble understanding... "...how scribes could allow themselves to bring in here and there changes which were not simply verbal ones, but such as materially affected the very meaning and, what is worse still, did not shrink from cutting out a passage or inserting one." (. Alterations to the Sinai Bible, Dr Constantin von Tischendorf, 1863, available in the British Library, London)

After years of validating the fabricated nature of the New Testament, a disillusioned Dr Tischendorf confessed that modern-day editions have "been altered in many places" and are "not to be accepted as true" (When Were Our Gospels Written?, Dr Constantin von Tischendorf, 1865, British Library, London).

Just what is Christianity?

The important question then to ask is this: if the New Testament is not historical, what is it? Dr Tischendorf provided part of the answer when he said in his 15,000 pages of critical notes on the Sinai Bible that "it seems that the personage of Jesus Christ was made narrator for many religions".

This explains how narratives from the ancient Indian epic, the Mahabharata, appear verbatim in the Gospels today (e.g., Matt. 1 :25, 2:1 1 , 8:1-4, 9:1-8, 9:18-26), and why passages from the Phenomena of the Greek statesman Aratus of Sicyon (271-213 BC) are in the New Testament.

Extracts from the Hymn to Zeus, written by Greek philosopher Cleanthes (c. 331-232 BC), are also found in the Gospels, as are 207 words from the Thais of Menander (c. 343-291), one of the "seven wise men" of Greece. Quotes from the semi-legendary Greek poet Epimenides (7th or 6th century BC) are applied to the lips of Jesus Christ, and seven passages from the curious Ode of Jupiter (c. 150 BC; author unknown) are reprinted in the New Testament.

Tischendorfs conclusion also supports Professor Bordeaux's Vatican findings that reveal the allegory of Jesus Christ derived from the fable of Mithra, the divine son of God (Ahura Mazda) and messiah of the first kings of the Persian Empire around 400 BC. His birth in a grotto was attended by magi who followed a star from the East. They brought "gifts of gold, frankincense and myrrh" (as in Matt. 2:1 1) and the newborn baby was adored by shepherds. He came into the world wearing the Mithraic cap, which popes imitated in various designs until well into the 15th century.

Mithra, one of a trinity, stood on a rock, the emblem of the foundation of his religion, and was anointed with honey. After a last supper with Helios and 1 1 other companions, Mithra was crucified on a cross, bound in linen, placed in a rock tomb and rose on the third day or around 25 March (the full moon at the spring equinox, a time now called Easter after the Babylonian goddess Ishtar). The fiery destruction of the universe was a major doctrine of Mithraism-a time in which Mithra promised to return in person to Earth and save deserving souls. Devotees of Mithra partook in a sacred communion banquet of bread and wine, a ceremony that paralleled the Christian Eucharist and preceded it by more than four centuries.

Christianity is an adaptation of Mithraism welded with the Druidic principles of the Culdees, some Egyptian elements (the pre-Christian Book of Revelation was originally called The Mysteries of Osiris and Isis), Greek philosophy and various aspects of Hinduism.

Why there are no records of Jesus Christ

It is not possible to find in any legitimate religious or historical writings compiled between the beginning of the first century and well into the fourth century any reference to Jesus Christ and the spectacular events that the Church says accompanied his life. This confirmation comes from Frederic Farrar (1831-1903) of Trinity College, Cambridge: "It is amazing that history has not embalmed for us even one certain or definite saying or circumstance in the life of the Saviour of mankind ... there is no statement in all history that says anyone saw Jesus or talked with him. Nothing in history is more astonishing than the silence of contemporary writers about events relayed in the four Gospels." (The Life of Christ, Frederic W. Farrar, Cassell, London, 1874).

This situation arises from a conflict between history and New Testament narratives. Dr Tischendorf made this comment: "We must frankly admit that we have no source of information with respect to the life of Jesus Christ other than ecclesiastic writings assembled during the fourth century." (Codex Sinaiticus, Dr Constantin von Tischendorf, British Library, London).

There is an explanation for those hundreds of years of silence: the construct of Christianity did not begin until after the first quarter of the fourth century, and that is why Pope Leo X (d. 1 521) called Christ a "fable" (Cardinal Bembo: His Letters..., op. cit.).

Extracted from Nexus Magazine
Volume 14, Number 4 (June - July 2007)
PO Box 30, Mapleton Qld 4560 Australia

CHAPTER 13
The Secular Humanist Declaration

In 1980, many countries of the world signed the "Secular Humanist Declaration". A Secular Humanist Declaration was an argument for and statement of support for democratic secular humanism. The document was issued in 1980 by the Council for Democratic and Secular Humanism (CODESH), now the Council for Secular Humanism (CSH). Compiled by Paul Kurtz, it is largely a restatement of the content of the American Humanist Association's 1973 Humanist Manifesto II, of which he was co-author with Edwin H. Wilson. Both Wilson and Kurtz had served as editors of The Humanist, from which Kurtz departed in 1979 and thereafter set about establishing his own movement and his own periodical. His Secular Humanist Declaration was the starting point for these enterprises.

The manifesto is mainly important and relevant because 8 of the main countries on the world signed the Declaration.

Introduction

Secular humanism is a vital force in the contemporary world. It is now under unwarranted and intemperate attack from various quarters. This declaration defends only that form of secular humanism which is explicitly committed to democracy. It is opposed to all varieties of belief that seek supernatural sanction for their values or espouse rule by dictatorship. Democratic secular humanism has been a powerful force in world culture. Its ideals can be traced to the philosophers, scientists, and poets of classical Greece and Rome, to ancient Chinese Confucian society, to the Carvaka movement of India, and to other distinguished intellectual and moral traditions. Secularism and humanism were eclipsed in Europe during the Dark Ages, when religious piety eroded humankind's confidence in its own powers to solve human problems. They reappeared in force during the Renaissance with the reassertion of secular and humanist values in literature and the arts, again in the sixteenth and seventeenth centuries with the development of modern science and a naturalistic view of the universe, and their influence can be found in the eighteenth century in the Age of Reason and the Enlightenment.

Democratic secular humanism has creatively flowered in modern times with the growth of freedom and democracy. Countless millions of thoughtful persons have espoused secular humanist ideals, have lived significant lives, and have contributed to the building of a more humane and democratic world. The modern secular humanist outlook has led to the application of science and technology to the improvement of the human condition. This has had a positive effect on reducing poverty, suffering, and disease in various parts of the world, in extending longevity, on improving transportation and communication, and in making the good life possible for more and more people. It has led to the emancipation of hundreds of millions of people from the exercise of blind faith and fears of superstition and has contributed to their education and the enrichment of their lives.

Secular humanism has provided an impetus for humans to solve their problems with intelligence and perseverance, to conquer geographic and social frontiers, and to extend the range of human exploration and adventure. Regrettably, we are today faced with a variety of anti-secularist trends: the reappearance of dogmatic authoritarian religions; fundamentalist, literalist, and doctrinaire Christianity; a rapidly growing and uncompromising Moslem clericalism in the Middle East and Asia; the reassertion of orthodox authority by the Roman Catholic papal hierarchy; nationalistic religious Judaism; and the reversion to obscurantist religions in Asia.

New cults of unreason as well as bizarre paranormal and occult beliefs, such as belief in astrology, reincarnation, and the mysterious power of alleged psychics, are growing in many Western societies. Full Disclosure: The author, Samuel Butler believes in reincarnation, and has known a good friend who was a famous psychic, who appeared on National Television (Mervin Griffin Show) as the best predictor of future events "available today". These disturbing developments follow in the wake of the emergence in the earlier part of the twentieth century of intolerant messianic and totalitarian quasi-religious movements, such as fascism and communism. These religious activists not only are responsible for much of the terror and violence in the world today but stand in the way of solutions to the world's most serious problems.

Paradoxically, some of the critics of secular humanism maintain that it is a dangerous philosophy. Some assert that it is "morally corrupting" because it is committed to individual freedom, others that it condones "injustice" because it defends democratic due process. We who support democratic secular humanism deny such charges, which are based upon misunderstanding and misinterpretation, and we seek to outline a set of principles that most of us share.

Secular humanism is not a dogma or a creed. There are wide differences of opinion among secular humanists on many issues. Nevertheless, there is a loose consensus with respect to several propositions. We are apprehensive that modern civilization is threatened by forces antithetical to reason, democracy, and freedom. Many religious believers will no doubt share with us a belief in many secular humanist and democratic values, and we welcome their joining with us in the defense of these ideals.

The manifesto is based on ten principles:
1. Free Inquiry
2. Separation of Church and State
3. The Ideal of Freedom
4. Ethics Based on Critical Intelligence
5. Moral Education
6. Religious Skepticism
7. Reason
8. Science and Technology
9. Evolution
10. Education

Free Inquiry
The first principle of democratic secular humanism is its commitment to free inquiry. We oppose any tyranny over the mind of man, any efforts by ecclesiastical, political, ideological, or social institutions to shackle free thought. In the past, such tyrannies have been directed by churches and states attempting to enforce the edicts of religious bigots. In the long struggle in the history of ideas, established institutions, both public and private, have attempted to censor inquiry, to impose orthodoxy on beliefs and values, and to excommunicate heretics and extirpate unbelievers. Today, the struggle for free inquiry has assumed new forms. Sectarian ideologies have become the new theologies that use political parties and governments in their mission to crush

dissident opinion. Free inquiry entails recognition of civil liberties as integral to its pursuit, that is, a free press, freedom of communication, the right to organize opposition parties and to join voluntary associations, and freedom to cultivate and publish the fruits of scientific, philosophical, artistic, literary, moral and religious freedom. Free inquiry requires that we tolerate diversity of opinion and that we respect the right of individuals to express their beliefs, however unpopular they may be, without social or legal prohibition or fear of sanctions. Though we may tolerate contrasting points of view, this does not mean that they are immune to critical scrutiny. The guiding premise of those who believe in free inquiry is that truth is more likely to be discovered if the opportunity exists for the free exchange of opposing opinions; the process of interchange is frequently as important as the result. This applies not only to science and to everyday life, but to politics, economics, morality, and religion.

Separation Of Church And State

Because of their commitment to freedom, secular humanists believe in the principle of the separation of church and state. The lessons of history are clear: wherever one religion or ideology is established and given a dominant position in the state, minority opinions are in jeopardy. A pluralistic, open democratic society allows all points of view to be heard. Any effort to impose an exclusive conception of Truth, Piety, Virtue, or Justice upon the whole of society is a violation of free inquiry. Clerical authorities should not be permitted to legislate their own parochial views – whether moral, philosophical, political, educational, or social – for the rest of society. Nor should tax revenues be exacted for the benefit or support of sectarian religious institutions. Individuals and voluntary associations should be free to accept or not to accept any belief and to support these convictions with whatever resources they may have, without being compelled by taxation to contribute to those religious faiths with which they do not agree. Similarly, church properties should share in the burden of public revenues and should not be exempt from taxation. Compulsory religious oaths and prayers in public institutions (political or educational) are also a violation of the separation principle. Today, nontheistic as well as theistic religions compete for attention. Regrettably, in communist countries, the power of the state is being used to impose an ideological doctrine on the society, without tolerating the expression of dissenting or heretical views. Here we see a modern secular version of the violation of the separation principle.

The Ideal Of Freedom

There are many forms of totalitarianism in the modern world — secular and non-secular — all of which we vigorously oppose. As democratic secularists, we consistently defend the ideal of freedom, not only freedom of conscience and belief from those ecclesiastical, political, and economic interests that seek to repress them, but genuine political liberty, democratic decision making based upon majority rule, and respect for minority rights and the rule of law. We stand not only for freedom from religious control but for freedom from jingoistic government control as well. We are for the defense of basic human rights, including the right to protect life, liberty, and the pursuit of happiness. In our view, a free society should also encourage some measure of economic freedom, subject only to such restrictions as are necessary in the public interest. This means that individuals and groups should be able to compete in the marketplace, organize free trade unions, and carry on their occupations and careers without undue interference by centralized political control. The right to private property is a human right without which other rights are nugatory. Where it is necessary to limit any of these rights in a democracy, the limitation should be justified in terms of its consequences in strengthening the entire structure of human rights.

Ethics Based On Critical Intelligence

The moral views of secular humanism have been subjected to criticism by religious fundamentalist theists. The secular humanist recognizes the central role of morality in human life; indeed, ethics was developed as a branch of human knowledge long before religionists proclaimed their moral systems based upon divine authority. The field of ethics has had a distinguished list of thinkers contributing to its development: from Socrates, Democritus, Aristotle, Epicurus, and Epictetus, to Spinoza, Erasmus, Hume, Voltaire, Kant, Bentham, Mill, G. E. Moore, Bertrand Russell, John Dewey, and others. There is an influential philosophical tradition that maintains that ethics is an autonomous field of inquiry, that ethical judgments can be formulated independently of revealed religion, and that human beings can cultivate practical reason and wisdom and, by its application, achieve lives of virtue and excellence. Moreover, philosophers have emphasized the need to cultivate an appreciation for the requirements of social justice and for an individual's obligations and responsibilities toward others. Thus, secularists deny that morality needs to be deduced from religious belief or that those who do not espouse a religious doctrine are immoral. For secular humanists, ethical conduct is, or should be, judged by critical reason, and their goal is to develop autonomous and responsible individuals, capable of making their own choices in life based upon an understanding of human behavior.

Morality that is not God-based need not be antisocial, subjective, or promiscuous, nor need it lead to the breakdown of moral standards. Although we believe in tolerating diverse lifestyles and social manners, we do not think they are immune to criticism. Nor do we believe that any one church should impose its views of moral virtue and sin, sexual conduct, marriage, divorce, birth control, or abortion, or legislate them for the rest of society. As secular humanists we believe in the central importance of the value of human happiness here and now. We are opposed to absolutist morality, yet we maintain that objective standards emerge, and ethical values and principles may be discovered, in the course of ethical deliberation. Secular humanist ethics maintains that it is possible for human beings to lead meaningful and wholesome lives for themselves and in service to their fellow human beings without the need of religious commandments or the benefit of clergy. There have been any number of distinguished secularists and humanists who have demonstrated moral principles in their personal lives and works: Protagoras, Lucretius, Epicurus, Spinoza, Hume, Thomas Paine, Diderot, Mark Twain, George Eliot, John Stuart Mill, Ernest Renan, Charles Darwin, Thomas Edison, Clarence Darrow, Robert Ingersoll, Gilbert Murray, Albert Schweitzer, Albert Einstein, Max Born, Margaret Sanger, and Bertrand Russell, among others.

Moral Education
We believe that moral development should be cultivated in children and young adults. We do not believe that any particular sect can claim

important values as their exclusive property; hence it is the duty of public education to deal with these values. Accordingly, we support moral education in the schools that is designed to develop an appreciation for moral virtues, intelligence, and the building of character. We wish to encourage wherever possible the growth of moral awareness and the capacity for free choice and an understanding of the consequences thereof. We do not think it is moral to baptize infants, to confirm adolescents, or to impose a religious creed on young people before they are able to consent. Although children should learn about the history of religious moral practices, these young minds should not be indoctrinated in a faith before they are mature enough to evaluate the merits for themselves. It should be noted that secular humanism is not so much a specific morality as it is a method for the explanation and discovery of rational moral principles.

Religious Skepticism

As secular humanists, we are generally skeptical about supernatural claims. We recognize the importance of religious experience: that experience that redirects and gives meaning to the lives of human beings. We deny, however, that such experiences have anything to do with the supernatural. We are doubtful of traditional views of God and divinity. Symbolic and mythological interpretations of religion often serve as rationalizations for a sophisticated minority, leaving the bulk of mankind to flounder in theological confusion. We consider the universe to be a dynamic scene of natural forces that are most effectively understood by scientific inquiry. We are always open to the discovery of new possibilities and phenomena in nature. However. we find that traditional views of the existence of God either are meaningless, have not yet been demonstrated to be true, or are tyrannically exploitative. Secular humanists may be agnostics, atheists, rationalists, or skeptics, but they find insufficient evidence for the claim that some divine purpose exists for the universe. They reject the idea that God has intervened miraculously in history or revealed himself to a chosen few or that he can save or redeem sinners. They believe that men and women are free and are responsible for their own destinies and that they cannot look toward some transcendent Being for salvation. We reject the divinity of Jesus, the divine mission of Moses, Mohammed, and other latter day prophets and saints of the various sects and denominations.

We do not accept as true the literal interpretation of the Old and New Testaments, the Koran, or other allegedly sacred religious documents, however important they may be as literature. Religions are pervasive sociological phenomena, and religious myths have long persisted in human history. In spite of the fact that human beings have found religions to be uplifting and a source of solace, we do not find their theological claims to be true. Religions have made negative as well as positive contributions toward the development of human civilization. Although they have helped to build hospitals and schools and, at their best, have encouraged the spirit of love and charity, many have also caused human suffering by being intolerant of those who did not accept their dogmas or creeds. Some religions have been fanatical and repressive, narrowing human hopes, limiting aspirations, and precipitating religious wars and violence. While religions have no doubt offered comfort to the bereaved and dying by holding forth the promise of an immortal life, they have also aroused morbid fear and dread. We have found no convincing evidence that there is a separable "soul" or that it exists before birth or survives death. We must therefore conclude that the ethical life can be lived without the illusions of immortality or reincarnation. Human beings can develop the self confidence necessary to ameliorate the human condition and to lead meaningful, productive lives.

Reason

We view with concern the current attack by nonsecularists on reason and science. We are committed to the use of the rational methods of inquiry, logic, and evidence in developing knowledge and testing claims to truth. Since human beings are prone to err, we are open to the modification of all principles, including those governing inquiry, believing that they may be in need of constant correction. Although not so naive as to believe that reason and science can easily solve all human problems, we nonetheless contend that they can make a major contribution to human knowledge and can be of benefit to humankind. We know of no better substitute for the cultivation of human intelligence.

Science And Technology

We believe the scientific method, though imperfect, is still the most reliable way of understanding the world. Hence, we look to the natural, biological, social, and behavioral sciences for knowledge of the universe and man's place within it. Modern astronomy and physics have opened up exciting new dimensions of the universe: they have enabled humankind to explore the universe by means of space travel. Biology and the social and behavioral sciences have expanded our understanding of human behavior. We are thus opposed in principle to any efforts to censor or limit scientific research without an overriding reason to do so. While we are aware of, and oppose, the abuses of misapplied technology and its possible harmful consequences for the natural ecology of the human environment, we urge resistance to unthinking efforts to limit technological or scientific advances. We appreciate the great benefits that science and technology (especially basic and applied research) can bring to humankind, but we also recognize the need to balance scientific and technological advances with cultural explorations in art, music, and literature.

Evolution

Today the theory of evolution is again under heavy attack by religious fundamentalists. Although the theory of evolution cannot be said to have reached its final formulation, or to be an infallible principle of science, it is nonetheless supported impressively by the findings of many sciences. There may be some significant differences among scientists concerning the mechanics of evolution; yet the evolution of the species is supported so strongly by the weight of evidence that it is difficult to reject it. Accordingly, we deplore the efforts by fundamentalists (especially in the United States) to invade the science classrooms, requiring that creationist theory be taught to students and requiring that it be included in biology textbooks. This is a serious threat both to academic freedom and to the integrity of the educational process. We believe that creationists surely should have the freedom to express their viewpoint in society. Moreover, we do not deny the value of examining theories of creation in educational courses on religion and the history of ideas; but it is a sham to mask an article of religious faith as a scientific truth and to inflict that doctrine on the scientific curriculum. If successful, creationists may seriously undermine the credibility of science itself.

Education

In our view, education should be the essential method of building humane, free, and democratic societies. The aims of education are many: the transmission of knowledge; training for occupations, careers, and democratic citizenship; and the encouragement of moral growth. Among its vital purposes should also be an attempt to develop the capacity for critical intelligence in both the individual and the community. Unfortunately, the schools are today being increasingly replaced by the mass media as the primary institutions of public information and education. Although the electronic media provide unparalleled opportunities for extending cultural enrichment and enjoyment, and powerful learning opportunities, there has been a serious misdirection of their purposes. In totalitarian societies, the media serve as the vehicle of propaganda and indoctrination. In democratic societies television, radio, films, and mass publishing too often cater to the lowest common denominator and have become banal wastelands. There is a pressing need to elevate standards of taste and appreciation. Of special concern to secularists is the fact that the media (particularly in the United States) are inordinately dominated by a pro religious bias. The views of preachers, faith healers, and religious hucksters go largely unchallenged, and the secular outlook is not given an opportunity for a fair hearing. We believe that television directors and producers have an obligation to redress the balance and revise their programming. Indeed, there is a broader task that all those who believe in democratic secular humanist values will recognize, namely, the need to embark upon a long term program of public education and enlightenment concerning the relevance of the secular outlook to the human condition.

Conclusion

Democratic secular humanism is too important for human civilization to abandon. Reasonable persons will surely recognize its profound contributions to human welfare. We are nevertheless surrounded by doomsday prophets of disaster, always wishing to turn the clock back

– they are anti-science, anti-freedom, anti-human. In contrast, the secular humanistic outlook is basically melioristic, looking forward with hope rather than backward with despair. We are committed to extending the ideals of reason, freedom, individual and collective opportunity, and democracy throughout the world community. The problems that humankind will face in the future, as in the past, will no doubt be complex and difficult. However, if it is to prevail, it can only do so by enlisting resourcefulness and courage. Secular humanism places trust in human intelligence rather than in divine guidance. Skeptical of theories of redemption, damnation, and reincarnation, secular humanists attempt to approach the human situation in realistic terms: human beings are responsible for their own destinies. We believe that it is possible to bring about a more humane world, one based upon the methods of reason and the principles of tolerance, compromise, and the negotiations of difference. We recognize the need for intellectual modesty and the willingness to revise beliefs in the light of criticism. Thus consensus is sometimes attainable. While emotions are important, we need not resort to the panaceas of salvation, to escape through illusion, or to some desperate leap toward passion and violence. We deplore the growth of intolerant sectarian creeds that foster hatred. **In a world engulfed by obscurantism and irrationalism, it is vital that the ideals of the secular world not be lost. THAT IS MY SECULAR VISION.**

A Secular Humanist Declaration was drafted by Paul Kurtz, Editor, Free Inquiry.

Endorsements
A Secular Humanist Declaration has been endorsed by the following individuals:

(Although we who endorse this declaration may not agree with all its specific provisions, we nevertheless support its general purposes and direction and believe that it is important that they be enunciated and implemented. We call upon all men and women of good will who agree with us to join in helping to keep alive the commitment to the principles of free inquiry and the secular humanist outlook. We submit that the decline of these values could have ominous implications for the future of civilization on this planet.)

United States Of America
- George Abell (professor of astronomy, UCLA)
- John Anton (professor of philosophy, Emory University)
- Khoren Arisian (minister, First Unitarian Society of Minneapolis)
- Isaac Asimov (science fiction author)
- Paul Beattie (minister, All Souls Unitarian Church; president, Fellowship of Religious Humanism)
- H. James Birx (professor of anthropology and sociology, Canisius College)
- Brand Blanshard (professor emeritus of philosophy, Yale)
- Joseph L. Blau (Professor Emeritus of Religion, Columbia)
- Francis Crick (Nobel Prize Laureate, Salk Institute)
- Arthur Danto (professor of philosophy, Columbia University)
- Albert Ellis (executive director, Institute for Rational Emotive Therapy)
- Roy Fairfield (former professor of social science, Antioch)
- Herbert Feigl (professor emeritus of philosophy, University of Minnesota)
- Joseph Fletcher (theologian, University of Virginia Medical School)
- Sidney Hook (professor emeritus of philosophy, NYU, fellow at Hoover Institute)
- George Hourani (professor of philosophy, State University of New York at Buffalo)
- Walter Kaufmann (professor of philosophy, Princeton)
- Marvin Kohl (professor of philosophy, medical ethics, State University of New York at Fredonia)
- Richard Kostelanetz (writer, artist, critic)
- Paul Kurtz (Professor of Philosophy, State University of New York at Buffalo)
- Joseph Margolis (professor of philosophy, Temple University)
- Floyd Matson (professor of American Studies, University of Hawaii)
- Ernest Nagel (professor emeritus of philosophy, Columbia)
- Lee Nisbet (associate professor of philosophy, Medaille)
- George Olincy (lawyer)

- Virginia Olincy
- W. V. Quine (professor of philosophy, Harvard University)
- Robert Rimmer (novelist)
- Herbert Schapiro (Freedom from Religion Foundation)
- Herbert Schneider (professor emeritus of philosophy, Claremont College)
- B. F. Skinner (professor emeritus of psychology, Harvard)
- Gordon Stein (editor, The American Rationalist)
- George Tomashevich (professor of anthropology, Buffalo State University College)
- Valentin Turchin (Russian dissident; computer scientist, City College, City University of New York)
- Sherwin Wine (rabbi, Birmingham Temple, founder, Society for Humanistic Judaism)
- Marvin Zimmerman (professor of philosophy, State University of New York at Buffalo)

Canada
- Henry Morgentaler (physician, Montreal)
- Kai Nielsen (professor of philosophy, University of Calgary)

France
- Yves Galifret (executive director, Union Rationaliste)
- Jean Claude Pecker (professor of astrophysics, College de France, Academie des Sciences)

Great Britain
- Sir A.J. Ayer (professor of philosophy, Oxford University)
- H.J. Blackham (former chairman, Social Morality Council and British Humanist Association)
- Bernard Crick (professor of politics, Birkbeck College, London University)
- Sir Raymond Firth (professor emeritus of anthropology, University of London)
- James Herrick (editor, The Free Thinker)
- Zheres A. Medvedev (Russian dissident; Medical Research

Council)
- Dora Russell (Mrs. Bertrand Russell) (author)
- Lord Ritchie Calder (president, Rationalist Press Association)
- Harry Stopes-Roe (senior lecturer in science studies, University of Birmingham; chairman, British Humanist Association)
- Nicholas Walter (editor, New Humanist)
- Baroness Barbara Wootton (Deputy Speaker, House of Lords)

India

- B. Shah (president, Indian Secular Society; director, Institute for the Study of Indian Traditions)
- V. M. Tarkunde (Supreme Court Judge, chairman, Indian Radical Humanist Association)

Israel

- Shulamit Aloni (lawyer, member of Knesset, head of Citizens Rights Movement)

Norway

- Alastair Hannay (professor of philosophy, University of Trondheim)

Yugoslavia

- Milovan Djilas (author, former vice president of Yugoslavia)
- M. Markovic (professor of philosophy, Serbian Academy of Sciences & Arts and University of Belgrade)
- Svet. Stojanovic (professor of philosophy, University of Belgrade)

From:
www.wikipedia.com
www.secularhumanism.org

SAMUEL BUTLER

CHAPTER 14
The genocides

List of genocides by death toll

The term genocide is contentious and its academic definition varies. This list only considers mass killings recognized as genocides by the legal definition in significant scholarship and criteria by the UN Genocide Convention.

This list of genocides by death toll includes death toll estimates of all deaths that are either directly or indirectly caused by genocide. It does not include non strictly-genocidal mass killing (variously called mass murder, crimes against humanity, politicide, policide, classicide, war crimes) such as the Thirty Years War (7.5 million deaths), Japanese war crimes (3 to 14 million deaths), the Atrocities in the Congo Free State (1 to 15 million deaths), the Great Purge (0.6 to 1.75 million death), or the Great Leap Forward (15 to 55 million deaths).

The United Nations Genocide Convention defines genocide as "acts committed with intent to destroy, in whole or in part, a national, ethnical, racial or religious group".[1] Various other definitions can be found in scholarly literature and national law of different countries.

Event	Location	From	To	Lowest estimate	Highest estimate	Proportion of group killed
The Holocaust[N 1] during World War II	German-occupied Europe	1941	1945	5,750,000 [3]	17,000,000 [4]	Around 2/3 of the Jewish population of Europe killed. Highest estimate includes 2 to 3 million Soviet POW's.[5]
Holodomor (Голодомор)[N 2] (Ukrainian genocide which is part of greater Soviet famine of 1932–33)	Ukrainian Soviet Socialist Republic, Soviet Union	1932	1933	1,800,000 [17][18][19][20]	7,500,000 [21][22][23][24][25]	Genocide of Ukrainians through artificial starvation by the Soviet regime.[26] At least 10% of Ukraine's population perished.[27] Its characterization as a genocide is disputed by some historians.[28][29]
Cambodian genocide[N 3]	Democratic Kampuchea	1975	1979	800,000 [38]	3,000,000 [33][39]	10–33% of total population of Cambodia killed[40][41] including: 100% of Cambodian Viets 50% of Cambodian Chinese and Cham 40% of Cambodian Lao and Thai 25% of Urban Khmer 16% of Rural Khmer
Kazakh genocide during the Soviet famine of 1932–33[N 4]	Kazakh Soviet Socialist Republic, Soviet Union	1931	1933	1,300,000 [42]	1,750,000 [43]	Some historians assume that 42% of the entire Kazakh population died in the famine.[43] The two Soviet census show that the number of the Kazakhs in Kazakhstan dropped from 3,637,612 in 1926 to 2,181,520 in 1937.[44]
Armenian genocide Մեծ Եղեռն (Medz Yeghern, "Great Crime")[N 5]	Ottoman Empire (territories of present-day Turkey, Syria and Iraq)	1915	1922	700,000 [45]	1,800,000 [45]	At least 50% of Armenians in Turkey killed[45]
Rwandan genocide[N 6]	Rwanda	1994	1994	200,000 [47]	2,000,000 [47]	70% of Tutsis in Rwanda killed 1/3 of Twa in Rwanda killed 20% of Rwandan's total population killed
Zunghar genocide 准噶尔灭族 大屠杀 in the Zunghar Khanate[N 7]	Qing Dynasty (Dzungaria)	1755	1758	480,000 [51]	600,000 [51]	80% of 600,000 Zungharian Oirats killed
Circassian genocide[N 8]	Circassia, Caucasus	1864	1867	400,000 [64]	1,500,000 [65]	90% to 97% of total Circassian population perished and deported by the Russian forces.[66][67][68]
Genocide by the Ustaše including the Serbian genocide[N 9]	Independent State of Croatia (territories of present-day Croatia, Bosnia and Herzegovina and Serbian Syrmia)	1941	1945	357,000 [70][71]	600,000 [70][71][72]	Conservative estimates ranging between 200,000 and 500,000 Serbs killed by the Ustaše.[73][74][75][76] (See death toll of Serbian genocide)
Bangladesh genocide[N 10]	Bangladesh	1971	1971	300,000	3,000,000 [78][79]	4% of Bangladesh's total population killed[82] Over 20% of Bengali Hindus killed[81] (Using 1 to 3 million deaths figures)
Greek genocide including the Pontic genocide[N 11]	Ottoman Empire (territories of present-day Turkey)	1914	1922	289,000 [82]	750,000 [83]	

Event	Location	From	To	Lowest estimate	Highest estimate	Proportion of group killed
Assyrian genocide ܐܣ (Seyfo, "Sword")[N 12]	Ottoman Empire (territories of present-day Turkey, Syria and Iraq)	1915	1923	275,000 [84]	750,000 [84]	
Albigensian Crusade (Cathar genocide)	Languedoc, France	1209	1229	200,000 [85]	1,000,000 [86]	[N 13]
Aardakh[N 14] (Soviet deportation of Chechens and other Vainakh populations)	Soviet Union, North Caucasus	1944	1948	144,704 [98]	200,000 [99][96][97][94]	23.5% to almost 50% of total Chechen population killed[98][99][99][91][92]
Porajmos (Romani genocide)[N 15]	Nazi controlled Europe	1935	1945	130,000 [103]	500,000 [104][95]	25% of Romani people in Europe killed
Battle of Carthage (Punic genocide)[N 16]	Carthage (territories of present-day Tunis, Tunisia)	149 BC	149 BC	150,000 [111][108]	150,000	Population reduced from 500,000 to 55,000. 150,000 died in the fall of Carthage.[111]
Polish Operation of the NKVD (Polish genocide)	Soviet Union	1937	1938	111,091 [112]	111,091	[N 17]
Mass-killings of Jews during the White Terror (Genocide of Jews)[N 18]	what is now Ukraine and Russia	1918	1923	100,000 [122]	300,000 [122]	An estimated 100,000 to 150,000 Jews in Ukraine and southern Russia were killed in pogroms perpetrated by Denikin's forces as well as Petlyura's nationalist-separatists.
Darfur genocide[N 19]	Darfur, Sudan	2003	ongoing	98,000 [125]	500,000 [126]	
East Timor genocide[N 20]	East Timor	1975	1999	85,320 [131]	196,720 [132]	13% to 44% of East Timor's total population killed (See death toll of East Timor genocide)
Burundian genocides of Hutus and Tutsis[N 21]	Burundi	1972	1993	80,000 [133][134] 50,000 [136]	210,000 [133][134] 50,000 [135]	
Libyan genocide[N 22]	Italian Libya	1923	1932	80,000 [146]	125,000 [147]	25% of Cyrenaican population killed[140]
Isaaq genocide[N 23]	Somalia	1988	1991	50,000 [163][153]	200,000 [164]	
Kurdish genocide[N 24]	Iraq	1986	1989	50,000 [167]	200,000 [168][169][169]	
Guatemalan genocide[N 25]	Guatemala	1962	1996	32,632 [174]	166,000 [173]	
Herero and Namaqua genocide[N 26]	German South-West Africa	1904	1908	34,000 [176]	110,000 [177][178]	60% (24,000 out of 40,000[175]) to 81.25% (65,000[179][180] out of 80,000[181]) of total Herero and 50%[176] of Nama population killed.
Latvian Operation of the NKVD (Latvian genocide)[N 27]	Soviet Union	1937	1938	16,573 [182]	16,573 [193]	
California genocide[N 28]	California	1846	1873	9,400 - 16,000 [184][185][186]	120,000 [186][196]	Amerindian population in California declined by 80% during the period
2017 Rohingya persecution[N 29]	Myanmar	2017	Present	9,000 - 13,700 [196]	43,000 [197]	
Bosnian genocide[N 30]	Bosnia and Herzegovina	1992	1995	8,373 [202]	31,107[203] 39,199 [204]	

Event	Location	From	To	Lowest estimate	Highest estimate	Proportion of group killed
Canadian residential school system (Canadian genocide)[N 31]	Canada[205]	1876	1996	3,201[206]	32,910[206]	
Selk'nam genocide[N 32]	Chile, Tierra del Fuego	Late 19th century	Early 20th century	2,500 [207]	3,900 [208]	84% The genocide reduced their numbers from around 3,000 to about 500 people. (Now pure Selk'nam are considered extinct.[208][209]
Genocide of Yazidis by ISIL[N 33]	northern Iraq and Syria	2014	present	2,100 [212]	4,400 [212][213]	
Black War (Genocide of Aboriginal Tasmanians)[N 34]	Tasmania, Australia	Mid 1820s	1832	400 [216]	1,000 [216]	

The Holocaust, also referred to as the Shoah, was the systematic, bureaucratic, state-organized, persecution and murder of approximately 6 million Jews by the German Nazi government and its collaborators. Initially it was carried out in German-occupied Eastern Europe by paramilitary death squads (Einsatzgruppen) by shooting or, less frequently, using ad hoc built gassing vans, and later in extermination camps by gassing.

By extending its definition the Holocaust may also refer to the other victims of German war crimes during the rule of Nazism, such as the Romani genocide's victims, Poles and other Slavic civilian populations and POWs, victims of Germany's eugenics program, political opponents, Homosexuals, Jehovah's Witnesses, and civil hostages and resisters from all over Europe.

In 2003 Holodomor, the man-made famine in Ukraine, was recognized by the United Nations as the result of actions and policies of the Soviet government of Joseph Stalin that caused millions of deaths, and in 2008 by the European Parliament as a crime against the Ukrainian people, and against humanity. Holodomor is considered a genocide in Ukraine, Australia, Canada, Colombia, Ecuador, Estonia, Georgia, Hungary, Latvia, Lithuania, Mexico, Paraguay, Peru, Poland, and Vatican City, while the Russian Federation views it as part of the wider Soviet famine of 1932-33. Scholars are divided and their debate is inconclusive on whether the Holodomor falls under the definition of genocide.

The Cambodian genocide was carried out by the Khmer Rouge led by Pol Pot who, planning to create a form of agrarian socialism founded on an extremist ideology coupled with ethnic hostility, forced

101

the urban population to relocate savagely to the countryside, among torture, mass executions, forced labor, and starvation.

The genocide ended in 1979 with the Cambodian invasion by the Vietnamese army. Up to 20,000 mass graves, the infamous Killing Fields, were uncovered, where at least 1,386,734 murdered victims found their final resting place. On 7 August 2014, two top leaders, Nuon Chea and Khieu Samphan, received life sentences for crimes against humanity.

Genocide of Kazakhs through artificial starvation by the USSR.
The extermination of the Armenians, carried out by the Young Turks, led to the coining of the word "genocide". It included massacres, forced deportations involving death marches, mass starvation, and occurred concurrently with the Assyrian and Greek genocides. The State of Turkey denies a genocide ever occurred.

Some 50 perpetrators of **the Rwandan genocide** have been found guilty by the International Criminal Tribunal for Rwanda, but most others have not been charged due to lack of witness accounts. Another 120,000 were arrested by Rwanda; of these, 60,000 were tried and convicted in the Gacaca court system. Perpetrators who fled into Zaire (Democratic Republic of the Congo) were used as a justification when Rwanda and Uganda invaded Zaire (First and Second Congo Wars). It is recognized by the international community as a genocide.

Zunghar genocide
The Manchu Qianlong Emperor of Qing China issued his orders for his Manchu Bannermen to carry out the genocide and eradication of the Zunghar nation, ordering the massacre of all the Zunghar men and enslaving Zunghar women and children. The Qianlong Emperor moved the remaining Zunghar people to the mainland and ordered the generals to kill all the men in Barkol or Suzhou, and divided their wives and children to Qing soldiers. The Qing soldiers who massacred the Zunghars were Manchu Bannermen and Khalkha Mongols. In an account of the war, Wei Yuan wrote that about 40% of the Zunghar households were killed by smallpox, 20% fled to Russia or the Kazakh Khanate, and 30% were killed by the army, leaving no yurts in an area of several thousands of Chinese miles except those of the surrendered.

Clarke wrote 80%, or between 480,000 and 600,000 people, were killed between 1755 and 1758 in what "amounted to the complete destruction of not only the Zunghar state but of the Zunghars as a people." Historian Peter Perdue has shown that the decimation of the Dzungars was the result of an explicit policy of extermination launched by the Qianlong Emperor. Although this "deliberate use of massacre" has been largely ignored by modern scholars, Mark Levene, a historian whose recent research interests focus on genocide, has stated that the extermination of the Dzungars was "arguably the eighteenth century genocide par excellence".

The Circassian genocide refers to the ethnic cleansing, massive annihilation, displacement, destruction and expulsion of the majority of the indigenous Circassians from historical Circassia, which roughly encompassed the major part of the North Caucasus and the northeast shore of the Black Sea. This occurred in the aftermath of the Caucasian War in the last quarter of the 19th century. The displaced people moved primarily to the Ottoman Empire. Former Russian President Boris Yeltsin's May 1994 statement admitted that resistance to the tsarist forces was legitimate, but he did not recognize "the guilt of the tsarist government for the genocide." In 1997 and 1998, the leaders of Kabardino-Balkaria and of Adygea sent appeals to the Duma to reconsider the situation and to issue the needed apology; to date, there has been no response from Moscow. In October 2006, the Adygeyan public organizations of Russia, Turkey, Israel, Jordan, Syria, the United States, Belgium, Canada and Germany have sent the president of the European Parliament a letter with the request to recognize the genocide against Adygean (Circassian) people.

On May 21, 2011, the Parliament of Georgia passed a resolution, stating that "pre-planned" mass killings of Circassians by Imperial Russia, accompanied by "deliberate famine and epidemics", should be recognized as "genocide" and those deported during those events from their homeland, should be recognized as "refugees". Georgia, which has poor relations with Russia, has made outreach efforts to North Caucasian ethnic groups since the 2008 Russo-Georgian War. Following a consultation with academics, human rights activists and Circassian diaspora groups and parliamentary discussions in Tbilisi in 2010 and 2011, Georgia became the first country to use the word "genocide" to refer to the events.

On 20 May 2011 the parliament of the Republic of Georgia declared in its resolution that the mass annihilation of the Cherkess (Adyghe) people during the Russian-Caucasian war and thereafter constituted genocide as defined in the Hague Convention of 1907 and the UN Convention of 1948.

Genocide by the Ustaše including the Serbian Genocide.

The government of the Independent State of Croatia murdered Serbs, Jews, Romani, and some dissident Croats and Bosniaks inside its borders, many in concentration camps, most notably Jasenovac camp. Ante Pavelić, the leader of the Ustaše, enacted racial laws similar to those of Nazi Germany, declaring Jews, Romani, and Serbs "enemies of the people of Croatia". He escaped to Spain after the war with the assistance of the Roman Catholic Church and fatally injured there some years later in an assassination attempt.

Bangladesh genocide.

Massacres, killings, rape, arson and systematic elimination of religious minorities (particularly Hindus), political dissidents and the members of the liberation forces of Bangladesh were conducted by the Pakistan Army with support from paramilitary militias—the Razakars, Al-Badr and Al-Shams—formed by the radical Islamist Jamaat-e-Islami party.

For the Greek genocide other sources give 450,000-900,000 casualties between Pontic, Cappadocian and Ionians Greeks. The genocide, instigated by the Ottoman government, included massacres, forced deportations involving death marches, summary expulsions, arbitrary executions, and destruction of Greek Orthodox cultural, historical and religious monuments.

The Assyrian genocide is commonly known as "Seyfo" (which means sword in Assyrian). It occurred concurrently with the Armenian and Greek genocides.

The Albigensian Crusade was a 20-year military campaign initiated by Pope Innocent III to eliminate Catharism, a Christian sect, in Languedoc, in southern France. The Catholic Church considered them heretics and ordered that they should be completely eradicated. Raphael Lemkin referred to the Albigensian Crusade as "one of the most conclusive cases of genocide in religious history". Kurt Jonassohn and Karin Solveig Björnson describe it as "the first ideological genocide."

Aardakh also known as Operation Lentil (Russian: Чечевица, Chechevitsa; Chechen: Вайнах махкахбахар Vaynax Maxkaxbaxar) was the Soviet expulsion of the whole of the Vainakh (Chechen and Ingush) populations of the North Caucasus to Central Asia during World War II. The expulsion, preceded by the 1940–1944 insurgency in Chechnya, was ordered on 23 February 1944 by NKVD chief Lavrentiy Beria after approval by Soviet Premier Joseph Stalin, as a part of Soviet forced settlement program and population transfer that affected several million members of non-Russian Soviet ethnic minorities between the 1930s and the 1950s.

The deportation encompassed their entire nations, well over 500,000 people, as well as the complete liquidation of the Chechen-Ingush Autonomous Soviet Socialist Republic. Hundreds of thousands of Chechens and Ingushes died or were killed during the round-ups and transportation, and during their early years in exile. The survivors would not return to their native lands until 1957. Many in Chechnya and Ingushetia classify it as an act of genocide, as did the European Parliament in 2004.

Porajmos (Romani pronunciation: IPA: [pʰoɽajˈmos]), or Samudaripen ("Mass killing"), the Romani genocide or Romani Holocaust, was the planned and attempted effort by the government of Nazi Germany and its allies to exterminate part of the Romani people of Europe. On 26 November 1935, a supplementary decree to the Nuremberg Laws stripping Jews of their German citizenship expanded the category "enemies of the race-based state" to include Romani, the same category as the Jews, and in some ways they had similar fates. In 1982, West Germany formally recognized that genocide had been committed against the Romani. In 2011, the Polish Government passed a resolution for the official recognition of 2 August as a day of commemoration of the genocide.

The massacre of Carthiginians (Punics) during their defeat by the Roman Republic is considered a genocide by many scholars.

The Polish Operation of the NKVD was a mass murder specifically aimed at the Polish ethnic group in the USSR by the orders of Soviet leader Joseph Stalin. Historian Michael Ellman asserts that the 'national operations', particularly the 'Polish operation', may constitute genocide as defined by the UN convention. His opinion is shared by Simon Sebag Montefiore, who calls the Polish operation of the NKVD 'a mini-genocide. Polish writer and commentator, Dr Tomasz Sommer, also refers to the operation as a genocide, along with Prof. Marek Jan Chodakiewicz among others.

It refers to the Jews in Ukraine and southern Russia were killed in pogroms perpetrated by Anton Denikin's armies as well as Petlyura's nationalist-separatists during the White Terror campaign of the Russian Civil War.

The Darfur genocide refer to the war crimes and crimes against humanity such as massacre and genocidal rape that occurred within the Darfur region during the War in Darfur perpetrated by Janjaweed militias and the Sudanese government. These atrocities have been called the first genocide of the 21at century. Sudan's president Omar al-Bashir has been indicted for his role in the genocide by the United Nations.

The East Timor genocide refers to the "pacification campaigns" of state sponsored terror by the Indonesian government during their occupation of East Timor. Oxford University held an academic consensus calling the Indonesian Occupation of East Timor genocide and Yale university teaches it as part of their "Genocide Studies" program. Precise estimates of the death toll are difficult to determine.

The 2005 report of the UN's Commission for Reception, Truth and Reconciliation in East Timor (CAVR) reports an estimated minimum number of conflict-related deaths of 102,800 (+/- 12,000). Of these, the report says that approximately 18,600 (+/- 1,000) were either killed or disappeared, and that approximately 84,000 (+/- 11,000) died from hunger or illness in excess of what would have been expected due to peacetime mortality. These figures represent a minimum conservative estimate that CAVR says is its scientifically-based principal finding.

The report did not provide an upper bound, however, CAVR speculated that the total number of deaths due to conflict-related hunger and illness could have been as high as 183,000. The truth commission held Indonesian forces responsible for about 70% of the violent killings.

Burundian genocide
In the long sequence of civil fights that occurred between Tutsi and Hutu since Burundi's independence in 1962, the 1972 mass killings of Hutu by the Tutsi and the 1993 mass killings of Tutsis by the majority-Hutu populace are both described as genocide in the final report of the International Commission of Inquiry for Burundi presented to the United Nations Security Council in 1996.

The Pacification of Libya, also known as the Libyan Genocide or Second Italo-Senussi War, was a prolonged conflict in Italian Libya between Italian military forces and indigenous rebels associated with the Senussi Order that lasted from 1923 until 1932, when the principal Senussi leader, Omar Mukhtar, was captured and executed. The pacification resulted in mass deaths of the indigenous people in Cyrenaica—one quarter of Cyrenaica's population of 225,000 people died during the conflict. Italy committed major war crimes during the conflict; including the use of chemical weapons, episodes of refusing to take prisoners of war and instead executing surrendering combatants, and mass executions of civilians. Italian authorities committed ethnic cleansing by forcibly expelling 100,000 Bedouin Cyrenaicans, half the population of Cyrenaica, from their settlements that were slated to be given to Italian settlers.

Italy apologized in 2008 for its killing, destruction and repression of the Libyan people during the period of colonial rule, and went on to say that this was a "complete and moral acknowledgement of the damage inflicted on Libya by Italy during the colonial era."

The Isaaq genocide or "Hargeisa Holocaust" was the systematic, state-sponsored massacre of Isaaq civilians between 1988 and 1991 by the Somali Democratic Republic under the dictatorship of Siad Barre. The number of civilian deaths in this massacre is estimated to be between 50,000–100,000 according to various sources, while local reports estimate the total civilian deaths to be upwards of 200,000 Isaaq civilians.

This included the leveling and complete destruction of the second and third largest cities in Somalia, Hargeisa (90 per cent destroyed) and Burao (70 per cent destroyed) respectively, and had caused 400,000 Somalis (primarily of the Isaaq clan) to flee their land and cross the border to Hartasheikh in Ethiopia as refugees, creating the world's largest refugee camp then (1988), with another 400,000 being internally displaced.

In 2001, the United Nations commissioned an investigation on past human rights violations in Somalia, specifically to find out if "crimes of international jurisdiction (i.e. war crimes, crimes against humanity or genocide) had been perpetrated during the country's civil war".

The investigation was commissioned jointly by the United Nations Co-ordination Unit (UNCU) and the Office of the United Nations High Commissioner for Human Rights. The investigation concluded with a report confirming the crime of genocide to have taken place against the Isaaqs in Somalia.

The Kurdish genocide also known as al-Anfal campaign (Arabic: حملة الأنفال), was a series of genocidal operations against the Kurdish people and other non-Arab populations in northern Iraq, that was led by the Ba'athist Iraqi President Saddam Hussein and was headed by Ali Hassan al-Majid in the final stages of the Iran–Iraq War.

The code name chosen by the former Iraqi Baathist government for this campaign takes its name from Surat al-Anfal, the eighth chapter of the Quran. The Anfal operations also targeted Assyrians, Shabaks, Iraqi Turkmens, Yazidis, Jews, Mandaeans, and many villages belonging to these ethnic groups were also destroyed. The Anfal campaign was recognized as a genocide by Norway, Sweden, the United Kingdom, and South Korea.

Guatemalan genocide
The government forces of Guatemala and allied paramilitary groups have been condemned by the Historical Clarification Commission for committing genocide against the Maya population and for widespread human rights violations against civilians during the civil war fought against various leftist rebel groups. At least an estimated 200,000 persons lost their lives by arbitrary executions, forced disappearances and other human rights violations. A quarter of the direct victims of human rights violations and acts of violence were women.

The Herero and Namaqua Genocide was the campaign to exterminate the Herero and Nama people that the German Empire undertook in German South-West Africa (modern-day Namibia). It is considered one of the first genocides of the 20th century.

The Lativian Operation refers to mass arrest and execution of Lativians during the Stalinist Great Purge.

The California genocide refers to the destruction of individual tribes like the Yuki people during the Round Valley Settler Massacres of 1856 - 1859, general massacres perpetrated by settlers chasing the gold rush against Indians like the Bloody Island Massacre, or Klamath River "War of Extermination" along with the overall decline of the Indian population of California due to disease and starvation exacerbated by the massacres.

The 2017 Rohingya persecution in Myanmar was a genocide against the Rohingya ethnic minority in Myanmar (Burma) by the Myanmar military and Buddhist extremists. The violence began on 25 August 2017 and has continued since, reaching its peak during the months of August and September in 2017.

The Rohingya people are a largely Muslim ethnic minority in Myanmar who have faced widespread persecution and discrimination for several decades. They are denied citizenship under the 1982 Myanmar nationality law, and are falsely regarded as Bengali immigrants by much of Myanmar's Bamar majority, to the extent that the government refuses to acknowledge the Rohingya's existence as a valid ethnic group.

The Arakan Rohingya Salvation Army (ARSA) is a Rohingya insurgent group that was founded in 2013 to "liberate [the Rohingya] people from dehumanising oppression". On 25 August 2017, ARSA claimed responsibility for coordinated attacks on police posts that reportedly killed twelve security forces. Myanmar's military forces immediately launched a series of retaliatory attacks against Rohingya civilians, and were joined by local Buddhist extremists.

Together they burnt down hundreds of Rohingya villages, killed thousands of Rohingya men, women, and children, tortured countless others, and sexually assaulted countless Rohingya women and girls. Several Rohingya refugees say they were forced to witness soldiers throwing their babies into burning houses to die in the fire. Numerous Rohingya refugee women and girls have provided accounts of being brutally gang raped. The violence has resulted in a refugee crisis, with an estimated 693,000 Rohingya fleeing to overcrowded refugee camps in the neighboring country of Bangladesh.

The Bosnian genocide comprises localized, in time and place, massacres like in Srebrenica and in Žepa committed by Bosnian Serb forces in 1995, as well as the scattered ethnic cleansing campaign throughout areas controlled by the Army of Republika Srpska during the 1992–95 Bosnian War. Srebrenica marked the most recent act of genocide committed in Europe and was the only theater of that war that fulfilled the definition of genocide as set by the International Criminal Tribunal for the former Yugoslavia (ICTY). On 31 March 2010, the Serbian Parliament passed a resolution condemning the Srebrenica massacre and apologizing to the families of Srebrenica for the deaths of Bosniaks ("Bosnian Muslims").

The Canadian residential school system was a network of boarding schools for Indigenous Canadian peoples. The school system was created for the purpose of removing children from the influence of their own culture and assimilating them into the dominant white Canadian culture. Over the course of the system's more than hundred-year existence, about 30% of Indigenous children (around 150,000) were placed in residential schools nationally. Many of these children died as a result.

The exact number of school related deaths remains unknown due to an incomplete historical record, though estimates posit at least 3,200 died as a result of being enrolled in the schools, with the highest figures estimating ten times that.

These schools harmed Indigenous children significantly by removing them from their families, depriving them of their ancestral languages, exposing many of them to physical and sexual abuse, and forcibly enfranchising them. Disconnected from their families and culture and forced to speak English or French, students who attended the residential school system often graduated unable to fit into either their communities or Canadian society. It ultimately proved successful in disrupting the transmission of Indigenous practices and beliefs across generations.

The legacy of the system has been linked to an increased prevalence of post-traumatic stress, alcoholism, substance abuse, and suicide, which persist within Indigenous communities today. In 2008, a Truth and Reconciliation Commission (TRC) was established to uncover the truth about the schools. In 2015, the TRC concluded with the establishment of the National Centre for Truth and Reconciliation, and the publication of a multi-volume report detailing the testimonies of survivors and historical documents from the time. The TRC report found that the school system amounted to cultural genocide.

The Selk'nam Genocide was the genocide of the Selk'nam people, indigenous inhabitants of Tierra del Fuego in South America, from the second half of the 19th to the early 20th century. Spanning a period of between ten and fifteen years the Selk'nam, which had an estimated population of some three thousand, saw their numbers reduced to 500.

The Genocide of Yazidis ' by ISIS includes mass killing, rape and enslavement of girls and women, forced abduction, indoctrination and recruitment of Yazidis boys (aged 7 to 15) to be used in armed conflicts, forced conversion to Islam and expulsion from their ancestral land. The United Nations' Commission of Inquiry on Syria officially declared in its report that ISIS is committing genocide against the Yazidis population. It is difficult to assess a precise figure for the killings but it is known that some thousands of Yazidis men and boys are still unaccounted for and ISIS genocidal actions against Yazidis people are still ongoing, as stated by the International Commission in June 2016.

The extinction of Aboriginal Tasmanians was called an archetypal case of genocide by Rafael Lemkin (coiner of the word genocide) among other historians, a view supported by more recent genocide scholars like Ben Kiernan who covered it in his book Blood and Soil: A History of Genocide and Extermination from Sparta to Darfur. This extinction also includes the Black War, which would make the war an act of genocide. Historians like Keith Windschuttle among other historians disagree with this interpretation in discourse known as the History wars.

From
en.wikipedia.org

ABOUT THE AUTHOR

Samuel Butler is a long time researcher on all the religions of the world and their origins.

His work on understanding how the religions of the world has become the source of wars, abuse and tyranny has produced several books like "**A curse on all their houses**" and his best seller "**Beyond all religion**".

Samuel Butler is being recognized for his new ideas about secularism and atheism in a new free thinking style.

He's now retired and occasionally plays golf on his free time.

INDEX

Pastor, 30
Paul, 10, 73, 74, 82, 92, 93
Pecker, 94
Pelides, 66
Penitent, 17
PENN, 58
Perdue, Peter, 103
Perpetrators, 102
Persian, 66, 79
Person A, 13, 14
Peru, 101
Pew Research Center, 27, 36
PITT, 56
Pokorsky, Jerry J., 24
Pol Pot, 101
Poland, 101
Poles, 101
Polish, vii, 105, 106
Pontic, 104
Pope Clement XIII, 77
Pope Innocent III, 104
Pope Leo X, 70, 80
Pope Sixtus V, 77
Porajmos, vii, 105
Presbyterial, 63
presbyters, 63, 64, 65, 66, 67, 68
priest, v, 22, 23
priests, 16, 22, 24, 66
Prime, 17
Princeton, 46, 93
Professor Telfer, 6
Propaganda, 76
prophets, 88, 91
Protagoras, 87
Protestant, 6
Protestants, 4
psychic, 83
Pulp Fiction, 58
Purge, 98, 109
Qianlong, 102

Made in the USA
Lexington, KY
03 April 2019